ANZUS IN REVISION
Changing Defense Features of Australia and New Zealand in the Mid-1980s

by

FRANK P. DONNINI, LT COL, USAF
Military Doctrine Analyst
Airpower Research Institute

Air University Press
Maxwell Air Force Base, Alabama 36112-5532

February 1991

Disclaimer

This publication was produced in the Department of Defense school environment in the interest of academic freedom and the advancement of national defense-related concepts. The views expressed in this publication are those of the author and do not reflect the official policy or position of the Department of Defense or the United States government.

This publication has been reviewed by security and policy review authorities and is cleared for public release.

Library of Congress Cataloging-in-Publication Data

Donnini, Frank P.
   ANZUS in revision: changing defense features of Australia and New Zealand in the mid-1980s /by Frank P. Donnini.
   p. cm.
   "February 1991."
   Includes bibliographical references (p.) and index.
   1. ANZUS Council. 2. Australia—Military relations—United States. 3. United States—Military relations—Australia. 4. Australia—Military relations—New Zealand. 5. New Zealand—Military relations—Australia. 6. United States—Military relations—New Zealand. 7. New Zealand—Military relations—United States. I. Title.
UA870.D66 1991
355′.033094—dc 20   90-28081
                                                                                                                                    CIP

Contents

Illustrations

Foreword

The post-World War II collective security network provided a foundation for Western allies and friends to deter aggression, contain communism, and promote the global cause of freedom and democracy, security, and peace. For more than 35 years, one successful part of the network was the "showcase" ANZUS defense alliance, a special and functional relationship between three close allies—Australia, New Zealand, and the United States.

ANZUS worked well because it allowed each partner to have a major say in matters that concerned all three and other players as well. It was synonymous with fair burden-sharing, mutual confidence, broad cooperation, and alliance unity. In military and intelligence matters, Australia and New Zealand were both self-reliant and dependent upon the United States.

In the mid-1980s, events caused the alliance to revise in such a way that a return to its former state became doubtful. In addition, Australia and New Zealand wanted their defense forces more self-reliant and increasingly focused on their own region. As a result, no one knew what a revised ANZUS and the shifting defense features of Australia and New Zealand really meant for themselves, the region, America, and Western security.

Lt Col Frank P. Donnini has helped increase our understanding by producing a definitive volume on *ANZUS in Revision: Changing Defense Features of Australia and New Zealand in the Mid-1980s*. It is a seminal work of real value, because he discusses the many issues involved with an open-minded, balanced approach that gives equal due to each ANZUS nation.

Colonel Donnini brings a unique perspective to the topic. As an intelligence officer in the early 1980s, he served on exchange with the Royal Australian Air Force in Canberra, Australia. While "down under," he observed and worked with all elements of the Australian and New Zealand military and intelligence organizations. As an Air Force research associate in the mid-1980s, he spent a year at the University of Pittsburgh researching, documenting, and writing this study. Finally, as a political-military affairs officer assigned to the Airpower Research Institute serving as a military doctrine analyst in the late 1980s, he produced the final refined product.

This excellent book will provide readers within each ANZUS country a much better understanding of the recent revisions in the West's "showcase" alliance and what is likely to happen now, especially in the Australian and New Zealand defense establishments. Accordingly, people in government, defense, and academia, who are concerned with such military and security matters, will want to read it.

DENNIS M. DREW, Colonel, USAF
Director, Airpower Research
Institute

About the Author

Lt Col Frank P. Donnini researched and wrote the bulk of this study while assigned as the 1986-87 Air Force research associate in visiting faculty status at the Graduate School of Public and International Affairs, University of Pittsburgh, Pennsylvania.

Colonel Donnini is a 1970 graduate of Union College, Schenectady, New York, with a BA in history, a 1977 graduate of Golden Gate University with a master's degree in public administration, a 1988 graduate of Creighton University with a master's degree in international relations, and a candidate for a doctorate in public administration from the University of Alabama. He received his commission through the Air Force ROTC program. He has completed Squadron Officer School, Air Command and Staff College, and Air War College.

A career intelligence officer, Colonel Donnini has served in a variety of intelligence assignments in the continental United States and overseas. He graduated from Target Intelligence and Photo/Radar Interpretation Officer courses.

His interest in the Australia, New Zealand, United States (ANZUS) defense alliance, the Australian and New Zealand defense forces, and the Southwest Pacific region began with his 1981-83 tour as an exchange officer with the Royal Australian Air Force (RAAF) in Canberra, Australian Capitol Territory, Australia. While there, he was the commander of the RAAF Target Intelligence Centre.

From 1987 to 1990, Colonel Donnini was assigned to Air University as a military doctrine analyst in the Airpower Research Institute of the Center for Aerospace Doctrine, Research, and Education (CADRE) at Maxwell AFB, Alabama. He is currently serving as chief of the Targets Division, Headquarters Tactical Air Command, Langley AFB, Virginia.

Acknowledgments

This study began while I was an Air Force research associate (RA) at the Graduate School of Public and International Affairs, University of Pittsburgh. It was a most rewarding experience for me both professionally and personally. During the 1986-87 academic year, I was a visiting faculty member conducting scholarly research in a very open and unstructured academic environment. I thank the US Air Force for providing me the opportunity to produce an in-depth independent study of security interest and to interact with the faculty, students, and staff of an excellent graduate school in a great university.

Many individuals were very helpful and supportive of my research efforts. I could never have accomplished this study without them. Fortunately during the year I was able to meet and interview numerous people in senior-level and staff-level diplomatic and defense positions in Washington, D.C., and Honolulu, Hawaii. Since their comments and opinions were not for attribution, I must thank them collectively for their time and effort. Special appreciation goes to those foreign service and military professionals at the Australian and New Zealand embassies in Washington.

I am very grateful to several people then associated with Air Force research and writing programs on the Air Staff at the Pentagon. These include Col Timothy Kline, chief of the Doctrine and Concepts Division, and Lt Col Don Drenth, head of the RA program and my predecessor as a research associate at the University of Pittsburgh. I must also give special thanks to Dr I. B. Holley, Jr., major general, USAFR, Retired, of Duke University for his invaluable insight into the right way to conduct solid research and for his advice during the RA orientation and the midtour seminars. Whenever I began to get off track, I referred to his notes on research and that always helped to straighten me out. In the Center for Aerospace Doctrine, Research, and Education at Air University, I am indebted to Col Dennis M. Drew; Dr David MacIsaac, Lt Col, USAF, Retired; and Dr Lawrence E. Grinter—all of the Airpower Research Institute—and Dr Richard Bailey of the Air

University Press for their constructive advice, editorial comments, and strong support.

On the academic side, many people deserve my sincere appreciation. These include Dr Henry S. Albinski and Prof Robert A. Brand of the Australian-New Zealand Studies Center, Pennsylvania State University; Dr Dora Alves of the National Defense University in Washington; and Dr Thomas-Durell Young, an independent scholar also based in Washington. Dora and Tom were especially generous in providing me advice, materials, and support throughout the whole research year. At the Graduate School of Public and International Affairs, Dean Lawrence J. Korb and Dr Donald M. Goldstein, Lt Col, USAF, Retired, were always there for support and friendship. Thanks also go to Joseph Cafaro for his great patience and skill in providing me initial word-processing support.

Last but by no means least, I want to extend real gratitude to my family for their complete support and encouragement on what began as a very interesting—and sometimes trying—year away from the Air Force and then became several years of finishing up what I had started. I have not said this often enough, but to my wife Zell and sons Zachary and Joshua, I thank you for everything now and in the future.

FRANK P. DONNINI, Lt Col, USAF
Military Doctrine Analyst
Airpower Research Institute

Introduction

Beginning in 1951 the defense features of Australia, New Zealand, and the United States (ANZUS)—operating together and alone—helped to produce a situation that brought security and stability to the vast South and Southwest Pacific regions. This alliance provided the foundation for Western security in the region. Many observers considered the trilateral and asymmetrical defense alliance of close allies a "showcase." Its success was such that the entire area, encompassing more than 10 percent of the earth's surface, was often called "Lake ANZUS."

However, events and occurrences from the mid-1980s onward have created significant adjustments and serious disturbances in the security arrangement. For example, much-publicized antinuclear policies, including New Zealand's ban on nuclear-powered and nuclear-weapons-carrying ships from port visits, and increases in external and internal destabilizing factors are threatening stability in the once quiet and exclusively Western region. At the same time, Australia and New Zealand are undergoing major changes in their conventional defense features as they strive for greater defense self-reliance and increased independence from the third partner in the alliance, the United States. If done as intended, the changing Australian and New Zealand defense features will enhance and improve the strong and capable deterrent force structures of the allies and provide real contributions to regional security and stability. Yet major problems are present that call into question not only the basic existence of ANZUS itself but also the transitioning defense capabilities and objectives of the countries concerned.

The cumulative impact of New Zealand posture and shifts, American reaction and concern, Australian changes and involvement, and political and economic nuances have resulted in unprecedented regional turmoil among the three countries. To date there has been little spillover elsewhere. Nevertheless, disturbances to established ways and means caused considerable discussion and debate on what has taken place and what its meaning is for future regional stability. This research study thus explores and answers a basic question: What effects do the recent shifts in Australian and New Zealand defense features and security conditions have on those countries, the United States, and the region in the revised ANZUS era?

The nature of ANZUS is revising both as an alliance for defense and a framework for security cooperation. For 35 years the successful ANZUS partnership was a major reason for the region's Western orientation and stability. Now the alliance is suddenly quite different from what it was just a few years ago, and its future is unknown. New Zealand is no longer an active partner; Australia is forced to have an expensive middleman role; and the United States is frustrated in seeing a weakening of its global security network characterized by effective deterrence and cooperative allies.

The defense forces of Australia and New Zealand are both experiencing major shifts. Some of the changes are due to adjustments in the revised ANZUS framework. In Australia and New Zealand, even more changes result from major defense policy changes designed to achieve two long-established but little-acted-upon goals: increased defense self-reliance and more independence from a great power protector, formerly Great Britain and since World War II, the United States. Past dependence meant Australia and New Zealand often had to adjust their own defense requirements to support those of larger allied forces. The result sometimes was service overseas that was extensive and costly—in both resources and, more importantly, lives. The most recent example was involvement with the United States in the Vietnam War as part of the commitment to "forward defense."

The study mainly provides analysis and commentary of these recent and planned shifts in Australian and New Zealand defense features. Two settings are used for each country. The first setting, the older one, covers the years before 1986 in Australia and before 1984 in New Zealand. Within this setting are two subsections. One is a full-house ANZUS and the commonly provided defense contributions from each country. The other subsection is the individual Australian and New Zealand defense contributions, ANZUS aside.

The second setting involves two time periods starting in the mid-1980s. For Australia it begins in 1986, a year highlighted by the Labor government-directed force structure study, *Review of*

Australia's Defence Capabilities, produced by Paul Dibb. This study was followed in 1987 by the government white paper on defense policy, *The Defence of Australia 1987*. The transitional year for New Zealand was 1984, when David Lange's Labour government was first elected to power. Subsequent to the election was an intense two-year debate cycle finalized by the 1987 government publication of its white paper on defense policy, *Defence of New Zealand — Review of Defence Policy 1987*.

The second setting also has two subsections. The first covers a partial or revised ANZUS and the commonly provided defense contributions, in spite of the absence of New Zealand. The other subsection details the individual Australian and New Zealand contributions to defense features, ANZUS aside. The second setting in each chapter contains more detail than the first, since it discusses present and future military service capabilities, defense problems, and other aspects of the complex defense relationships.

While recognizing the many security and related benefits derived from the close relationship with the United States, a growing number of concerned Australians and New Zealanders now want to reorient defense policies more toward their areas of direct strategic importance and interest—the South and Southwest Pacific regions. Thus, whatever their outcomes, the ongoing and projected changes in Australian and New Zealand conventional defense features become more significant in regards to Western security. In the revised ANZUS era, American interests and objectives in the region also are affected by such changes.

Several means are available for the former close allies to reverse the growing negative aspects of collective security in the region and to work together again in an operative and positive defense arrangement. Suggested changes in defense and policy options involve all three ANZUS nations, with the United States having the primary role. Evidence indicates that the United States must be more attentive and supportive to the region, the American and Australian bilateral defense relationship must become stronger, Australian defense features must improve as the country attempts to assert its role as a regional middle power, and New Zealand's defense capabilities will decline further unless improvements occur soon.

To place changing Australian and New Zealand defense features in proper context, a discussion of the ANZUS alliance itself is necessary. A broad-based comment on its present status in an evolving region of growing importance and problems is presented. Following that is a more substantive look at the alliance, tracing its development and wide-ranging impact for the three allies and the Lake ANZUS region.

Chapter 1

ANZUS in Revision

Defense strategy for the East Asia-Pacific region is based on forward deployed US forces, robust alliances, and self-sufficient friends.

—Caspar Weinberger, US Secretary of Defense, 1985

Few can deny that the Australia, New Zealand, and the United States (ANZUS) trilateral alliance, if not in disarray, was at least quite different in the mid-1980s from the "showcase" it once was. The formerly solid, cost-effective, and asymmetrical Western defense alliance is now in a state of revision: two bilateral agreements have replaced the former successful arrangement. One agreement has the United States and Australia working closely together in a variety of security-related matters under the cloak of a "revised ANZUS," which constitutes Australia's single most important bilateral relationship. The other agreement has brought about an increase in Australian and New Zealand defense cooperation. Regardless of the outcome of the structure of the once venerable alliance, a return to its former business-as-usual approach and close cooperative relationship is doubtful. Too much has occurred and has been said in the last few years to expect such a turnaround. Perhaps these latest problems are only manifestations of deep and continuing weaknesses within ANZUS that were finally brought to a head. Some observers believe that the flexible and nonbinding ANZUS Treaty reflects Western thinking of a generation ago and has outlived or outgrown its original usefulness.[1] By the late 1980s, the ANZUS defense alliance was clearly in trouble and at a possible crossroads of its existence. The changing defense features and security objectives for the region must be seen against this background.

American post-World War II policy toward the region has been characterized as one of benign neglect. American policymakers never intended to slight their allies in the South and Southwest Pacific, since maintaining the ANZUS partnership was a key US objective. US Secretary of Defense Caspar Weinberger described the long-standing partnership with Australia and New Zealand (the current difficulties with New Zealand, notwithstanding) as one of the five pillars of American defense policy in East Asia and the Pacific.[2] Despite this, reality dictated that other events and relationships in the larger East Asia-Pacific region (accompanying map) and extending into the Indian

East Asia and the Pacific

Source: US State Department map files, May 1984. Courtesy of Prof Robert Brand, Australian–New Zealand Studies Center, The Pennsylvania State University.

Ocean area were often more important and of greater concern for the advancement of US objectives and interests.

Besides, ANZUS traditionally provided a stable environment for the South and Southwest Pacific regions that allowed the United States to concentrate on other areas in East Asia and the Pacific. In 1985 when the alliance experienced a crisis and a number of security factors emerged, the United States slowly began to realize that more attention must be paid to the region and therefore renewed its emphasis there. To help maintain its Western dominance, the United States insisted that regional stability must consistently be a governing aspect of military, political, and economic policies. Yet the United States, a nation accustomed to strong and productive collective security arrangements, believed that it "cannot, and should not, go it alone."[3] With its many forms, the revised ANZUS structure has experienced powerful tremors that could jeopardize security in a region long considered to be one with few problems. The notion of the Southwest Pacific as an area of peace and serenity is no longer the norm.[4]

Increasing Regional Problems

The region has changed to the extent it is no longer, in the words of New Zealand Foreign Affairs Secretary Merwyn Norrish, simply a "tranquil backwater, secure in its isolation from unsettling and potentially hostile influences from abroad."[5] The area is beginning to have more instability. Although outright military invasion of Australia, New Zealand, or any other island-states and territories is unrealistic, other credible possibilities for problem creation exist.

Among external destabilizers to regional stability, the Soviet Union has assumed a greater role. Having formally announced intentions to be involved in the Pacific Basin affairs and in competition with the West, the Soviet Union has demonstrated its plans by expanding the size and power of its military forces in East Asia and the Pacific. A worrisome example close at hand to the Southwest Pacific region can be found in the increase of defensive and offensive assets the Soviets have placed at the Cam Ranh Bay naval facility and Da Nang air base in the Socialist Republic of Vietnam. When military options have not proved the best means to achieve objectives, the Soviets have tried economic and political inroads to accomplish the same. Fishing rights negotiations with economically vulnerable island-nations (first with Kiribati and now with Vanuatu) and political support for nuclear free zone issues have become useful starting points. Regardless of the future outcome of its actions, the Soviet Union has welcomed the weakening of the ANZUS alliance. Many believe the "Lake ANZUS" perception was a primary reason that influence in such a large region was denied to the Soviets for so long.[6]

A wide range of opinions exist concerning Soviet intentions and capabilities in the region. Extreme views have the Soviets able to strike and cause all kinds of problems in the future. Former Australian Prime Minister Malcolm Fraser said that Soviet presence would "first start as a fish processing facility, then some refueling facilities; [next, they] will require repair facilities [and], in turn, an airfield. Then it is a [Soviet military] base."[7] A US Navy admiral, testifying in a US congressional hearing on East Asia and the Pacific, felt strongly that Soviet long-range plans are to gain a military foothold in a strategically important region and to improve surveillance of the US missile test range at Kwajalein, in the adjacent Marshall Islands group.[8] Although their opinions appear farfetched—especially since the Soviets carry minimal weight in Australia, New Zealand, and the rest of the region—Soviet presence and efforts could possibly grow if the Soviets perceive a less influential ANZUS alliance or some similar-type arrangement. As one former US State Department official remarked, "Even if they are not in sight, bear in mind what the Soviet Union is about."[9]

Another destabilizing external factor involves potential problems with Indonesia, Australia's heavily populated neighbor to the near north. Because of its heritage of confrontation politics and present policies of "national resilience," Australia and New Zealand perceive Indonesia as the most difficult member of the Association for Southeast Asian Nations (ASEAN) with which to conduct relations. As a country straddling both the South Pacific and the Indian Ocean-Southeast Asia regions, Australia has special concerns. For some onlookers Indonesia could conceivably be the source of regional instability or provide the avenue through which it could come.[10]

Internal problems are increasing. Widespread antinuclear protests and a demand for a South Pacific nuclear free zone—also known as SPNFZ—may continue and likely will grow stronger. Even though much of the animosity and strong feelings are due to France and its continuing nuclear weapons testing in French Polynesia (in the Southeast Pacific), some strong feelings also are directed toward the other nuclear powers, most especially the United States—with its nuclear navy. Additionally, unsettling economic and migration difficulties affect the fragile South Pacific island-states. Political decolonization problems, such as those in New Caledonia, still beset some of France's last territorial holdings in the region. Even political and military coups are no longer unheard of, as evidenced by the 1987 events (with their racial overtones) in the island-nation of Fiji, once the model state of regional stability. It was the first coup ever in the South Pacific.[11]

New-Look Defense Features of Australia and New Zealand

Significant to the entire region are the changing conventional defense features of Australia and New Zealand. For years both nations talked about and tried to achieve national security objectives of greater self-reliance and more independence. While being both contributing and receiving members of ANZUS might have seemed contradictory, governments representing all major political parties within Australia and New Zealand felt such opposing concepts were worthwhile and attempted to balance them. Until recently real self-reliance and independence in defense matters were limited. As future guidelines for national defense efforts and directions, the defense white papers were significant documents.[12]

As the middle-size partner in ANZUS, Australia is a main Western security link overlapping the Southwest Pacific, Southeast Asia, and Indian Ocean regions. It has increased its primary role in the planned changes and future direction of regional security efforts. The 70,000-member Australian Defence Force (ADF) is a capable and professional military force, which has earned a deserved reputation for dependability and effectiveness, especially in wartime. If ANZUS as a genuine trilateral alliance ceases to exist, Australia plans to have a stronger and more effective bilateral defense relationship with the United States. The country also wants to be more self-reliant, despite its acknowledged dependence on and linkage with the United States—particularly in the important areas of capital systems acquisitions, logistics support, and intelligence information.

Several major events in the mid-1980s shaped the changing defense features of Australia. One of the most notable was the 1986 *Review of Australia's Defence Capabilities: Report to the Minister for Defence*, written by Paul Dibb for the Labor government of Prime Minister Bob Hawke and Defence Minister Kim Beazley. The review turned out to be a detailed, encompassing, and controversial examination of the future ADF structure. Following this report in 1987 was the comprehensive Labor government white paper, *The Defence of Australia 1987*, which laid out long-range defense policy by incorporating key points of the Dibb report and later American concerns and desires for collective security

The Australian people believe that their best warranty is an ability for Australia to defend itself and have an area security which is connected to world security. Thus Australia in its white paper realized that self-reliance must achieve four fundamental objectives in defense policy:

- maintain and develop a capacity for independent defense of Australia and its interests,
- promote strategic stability and security in the region,
- strengthen the ability to meet the mutual obligations shared with its chief allies: the United States and New Zealand, and
- enhance the ability, as a member of the Western association of nations, to contribute to strategic stability at the global level.[13]

As far as political and military leaders are concerned, the new overall Australian effort has potential and appears to be moving generally in the right direction. A number of key factors, acting alone or in combination, could seriously affect Australia's ability to provide for its considerable program of defense improvements and enhancements. These factors include budget limitations, service capabilities, logistics support, and retention of skilled personnel. The issue thus becomes whether the new defense features—that Australia is trying to achieve—are the best means to satisfy these important objectives.

New Zealand (by far the smallest partner in ANZUS and the main Western security influence in the South Pacific region, its area of direct strategic concern) is undergoing its own review of defense policies and improvements. Under the dominant leadership of Prime Minister David Lange, the New Zealand Labour government has changed significantly the way that country approaches its security and defense needs. The government's expressed concentration is on self-reliance and a greater South Pacific regional conventional focus.

The country's past contributions to collective security and regional stability inside and outside ANZUS were proportional and useful. While the small country had minimal direct value in US strategic calculations, it was a close ally and a contributing member of the showcase alliance. However, recent postures and policies have challenged American foreign policy in unprecedented ways.[14] A changing political climate—influenced by sustained antinuclear attitudes and initiatives in New Zealand and the region—and economic constraints are responsible for shifting the country's defense assets away from the revising ANZUS formal and informal arrangements.

A comprehensive debate cycle on national defense was finalized after two years with the Labour government's publication in 1987 of a white paper on defense policy. Unlike its Australian counterpart, the New Zealand white paper is very politicized in content and tone. The central objective of the defense policy is to preserve New Zealand's security and interests. This approach is sensible and acceptable, but the policy goes on to state:

> For the first time, we have adopted in formal policy terms the concept that the New Zealand armed forces will have a capability to operate independently, although more probably in concert with Australia, to counter low level contingencies in our region of direct strategic concern.[15]

Problems begin here. Despite the rhetoric and intentions, the 12,000-member New Zealand Defence Forces appear to be steadily declining in capability and effectiveness. Consequences of the continuing and abrupt defense changes will alter in unknown ways the defense feature look of New Zealand for a long time to come.

Notes

1. Henry S. Albinski, "Australia and New Zealand in the 1980s," *Current History* 85, no. 510 (April 1986): 154; idem, "Australia and the United States: Appraisal of the Relationship," *Australian Journal of Politics and History* 29, no. 2 (1983): 288; Owen Harries, "Crisis in the Pacific," *Commentary*, June 1985, 47, 50; Andrew Mack, "Crisis in the Other Alliance: ANZUS in the 1980s," *World Policy Journal* 3, no. 3 (Summer 1986): 459, 468.

2. Thomas-Durell Young, "United States Security Interests and Objectives" (paper presented at a security conference on Strategic Imperatives and Western Responses in the Pacific, Sydney, Australia, 9-12 February 1986), 47; Caspar W. Weinberger, "The Five Pillars of Our Defense Policy in East Asia and the Pacific," *Defense 84*, no. 23 (April 1984): 3. In addition to the partnership with Australia and New Zealand, the other four pillars are: the importance of the US security relationship with Japan, US commitment to stability on the Korean peninsula, the efforts to build up an enduring relationship with China, and the support for the political and economic vitality of ASEAN. (The ASEAN countries are Indonesia, Malaysia, Singapore, Thailand, the Philippines, and Brunei.)

3. William J. Crowe, "No 17—The US Cannot, and Should Not, Go It Alone," *Pacific Defence Reporter* 12, no. 2 (August 1985): 11. The theme Admiral Crowe repeatedly stressed then as commander in chief of the US Pacific Command and later as chairman of the Joint Chiefs of Staff was that Western allies have shared burdens and responsibilities.

4. Richard D. Fisher, "Responding to New Zealand's Challenge to Western Security in the South Pacific," *Backgrounder*, no. 48 (24 July 1986): 11; Richard Armitage as reported in Denis Warner, "No 2—'New Zealand Can't Have It Both Ways,'" *Pacific Defence Reporter* 11, no. 10 (April 1985): 14. Armitage's comments were similar to Weinberger's remarks one year earlier in "Five Pillars of Our Defense Policy in East Asia and the Pacific"; statement of Karl D. Jackson, deputy assistant secretary of defense for East Asia and Pacific Affairs, in House Committee on Foreign Affairs, *United States Policy toward New Zealand and Australia and the Current State of ANZUS: Hearings before the Subcommittee on Asian and Pacific Affairs*, 99th Cong., 2d sess., 25 September 1986, 2.

5. Merwyn Norrish as reported in Ian Templeton, "Wellington Ponders Post-ANZUS Pacific Security," *The Bulletin* 108, no. 5519 (20 May 1986): 104.

6. Quoted in Jill Smollowe, "Pacific Overtures: Moscow's Moves in the Far East Worry Washington," *Time* 128, no. 20 (17 November 1986): 58-59; Crowe, 14; quoted in B. Andrews, "Admiral Points to Soviet Fish Pact," *Washington Times*, 11 September 1986, 4-D; Jack V. Roome, "Soviet Military Expansion in the Pacific," *Pacific Defence Reporter* 13, no. 2 (August 1986): 13-14.

7. Quoted in Clyde Haberman, "Challenge in the Pacific," *New York Times*, 7 September 1986, 104.

8. Peter Samuel, "Soviets Buying Access to Strategic South Pacific Islands, Baker Tells Congress," *Defense News*, 29 September 1986, 13; Dora Alves, "Sea Change in the New Pacific," *Defense & Foreign Affairs* 15, no. 6 (June 1987): 41; Andrews, 4-D.

9. Quoted in Denis Warner, "Soviet Union Not Just a Country, But a Cause," *Pacific Defence Reporter* 12, no. 10 (April 1986): 10.

10. William T. Tow, "ANZUS and American Security," *Survival* 23, no. 6 (1981): 267; Dora Alves, *The ANZUS Partners*, Georgetown University Significant Issue Series 6, no. 8 (Washington, D.C.: Center for Strategic and International Studies, 1984), 48.

11. Alves, *The ANZUS Partners*, 15; Dora Alves, *Anti-nuclear Attitudes in New Zealand and Australia* (Washington, D.C.: National Defense University Press, 1985), 20, 26-29; "Fiji Coup to Block Indian Power," *Pittsburgh Press*, 17 May 1987, A-7.

12. *Defence of New Zealand: Review of Defence Policy 1987* (Wellington, New Zealand: V. R. Ward, Government Printer, February 1987); *The Defence of Australia 1987* (Canberra, Australia: Australian Government Publishing Service, March 1987).

13. *The Defence of Australia 1987*, vii, ix.

14. Albinski, "Australia and New Zealand in the 1980s," 154.

15. *Defence of New Zealand*, 5-6, 38.

Chapter 2

ANZUS—In Good Times and in Bad Times

Heart of the matter [is that] alliances can only succeed when founded in common interest. . . . It is not in New Zealand's interest to form part of a nuclear deterrent.

—David Lange, Labour Prime Minister of New Zealand

We [United States] might be pissed off with New Zealand, but Australia is a real friend.

—Marian Chambers, a senior official attached to US House of Representatives Foreign Affairs Committee

Until recently ANZUS (that special defense arrangement involving Australia, New Zealand, and the United States) was considered a showcase alliance. The characterization was especially valid when ANZUS was compared with the most visible and most important security alliance of the United States: the North Atlantic Treaty Organization (NATO). Although ANZUS did not have a formal staff like that of NATO and was far short of meeting the original Australian wish for a Pacific version of the North Atlantic alliance, it was still perceived by many to have been effective and efficient. Like NATO, ANZUS was a collective security pact in which the United States stated "it would act to meet the common danger in accordance with its constitutional processes." [1]

"Showcase" Alliance in a "No-Problem" Region

The American security guarantee for Australia and New Zealand was often a subject of debate "down under." The lack of any conceivable direct military threat to either of the two antipodean countries partly caused the discussion. Related also was the unknown US military force response if such an adversarial threat were ever to develop.

Apart from the security guarantee, Australia and New Zealand benefited from ANZUS in a number of ways:

- privileged access to American intelligence sources and information;
- purchase of US military technology and equipment, some of which was state of the art or close to it, on very favorable terms;
- opportunity to exercise and train on a regular basis with American armed forces;
- participation in a variety of conferences and forums;
- cooperation on defense science matters;
- sharing of operational doctrine and tactics; and
- personnel exchanges.

The Australian and New Zealand recipients valued these benefits and realized that many were irreplaceable. None of the benefits meant significant costs to the United States, which in turn also benefited from this special two-way and sometimes three-way flowing arrangement. In fact, for years ANZUS was cost-effective for all countries concerned.[2]

United States Alliance Perspectives

The United States saw ANZUS as a tribute to the collective strength and vigor of the Western system of interlocking defense alliances. Officials believed these alliances, when working together, were instrumental in deterring aggression and preventing the outbreak of large-scale conflict. Many of them also felt that alliances created mutually reinforcing links among national interests and security features of these Western-oriented nations.[3] Thus, ANZUS provided the United States not only a regional area in which its armed forces could exercise and operate but also an opportunity to devote elsewhere, when required, some of these same limited resources, since Australia and New

Zealand effectively stabilized the region with their own defense resources.

US Assistant Secretary of State for East Asia and the Pacific Paul D. Wolfowitz said that successful ANZUS alliance management depended on meeting five critical challenges. First, as an alliance of democracies, ANZUS had a need for foreign policy coherence. Sustaining public support for policies was essential. Second, an ongoing requirement existed for alliance partners to have extensive contacts at all levels of government and society. This requirement was most evident in senior consultation at the foreign ministry levels and in close defense cooperation on the military side. A key element of close defense cooperation had military forces working together, especially the three navies because of the maritime nature of the region. Third, long-term consistency and continuity were necessary. Fourth, each alliance member had to accept both the mutual burdens and benefits of ANZUS. These included joint (US and Australian) defense facilities in Australia, port and airfield access in Australia and New Zealand, standardization and interoperability efforts, and exchanges and consultations. From the US perspective, tangible evidence of treaty commitment was clear in the maintenance of an American presence in the region and the demonstration of an ability to operate effectively with treaty partners. The final challenge was to recognize that ANZUS, important though it was, was still only one part of a much larger and multifaceted relationship among the three countries.[4]

Other American Military Interests

For Americans, the ANZUS cooperative defense alliance caused other positive aspects that supported a wide range of military interests and objectives not specifically covered by the ANZUS Treaty. A glance at current arrangements involving each of the US military services provides tangible evidence.

Navy/Marines

Australia is frequently visited and generally well liked by US Navy and Marine Corps personnel. In 1986, for example, 57 naval ships visited the country, mostly in Western Australia. The port visits to Freemantle and Perth were so popular among the Americans—many of whom had just spent several months at sea—that they were designated the favorite rest and relaxation areas for US sailors and marines overseas. The American objective each year is to achieve a consistent four-to-five dozen US ship visits and a series of combined military exercises and training. If this goal is achieved, the United States feels it can continue playing a stabilizing role far beyond the immediate region.[5]

Air Force

The US Air Force has a variety of connections and interests in the region. Although not as extensive as the Navy's, they are still significant. Air Force ties with Australia traditionally have been strong. Senior leadership of both air forces have met on a regular basis throughout the years. There was a 20-year period of annual discussions between the US Air Force chief of staff and the chief of air staff of the Royal Australian Air Force (RAAF) called "airman-to-airman talks." These discussions ended in the early 1980s. Although varying levels of bilateral meetings, visits, and discussions continue, there have been some suggestions to renew the top-level formal arrangements.[6]

Air Force military transport aircraft have been regularly deployed to Australia with the primary purpose of supplying and supporting the US-Australian joint defense facilities. There is usually at least one Military Airlift Command (MAC) aircraft in the country at any given time.

Air-related exercises between the two air forces and other services also helped US interests. The largest air exercise is the Pitch Black series. Begun on a bilateral basis in 1984, these tactical air defense exercises have grown in scope and detail. When possible, the RAAF also sends its aircraft and personnel to US-sponsored Cope Thunder exercises in the Philippines and Red Flag exercises in the continental United States. Most participants on both sides find these exercises worthwhile and enhancing.

The USAF Strategic Air Command (SAC) not only participates in such exercises as Pitch Black but also has its own special training programs in Australia. The programs are called Busy Boomerang and Glad Customer. Busy Boomerang, SAC's first program, started around 1980. The idea is for SAC's B-52 heavy bomber aircraft to fly low-level routes over northern Queensland, Australia, but not to land on Australian territory. Most of these aircraft fly from and return to Andersen AFB, Guam. Busy Boomerang consists of several aerial training routes and provides the only good places for Air Force aircrews to practice terrain avoidance in the South Pacific region. Glad Customer, the second SAC program, started in early 1981 in Darwin. The Australian government gave permission for SAC to fly B-52H models and supporting KC-135 aerial tankers from RAAF Base Darwin for overwater navigation and maritime surveillance. These are primarily US Pacific Command support missions into the Indian Ocean. Busy Boomerang Delta, the third SAC program, has been in operation there since 1982. A cell of B-52s flies from Andersen AFB or the US mainland and lands at Darwin. Since November 1986 these aircraft have been able to fly missions in which they depart, fly, and then return to Darwin. The Australian government ostensibly approved this SAC program because it was cost-effective for the United States. The US (and SAC) position was to be appreciative of these special training arrangements.

Another USAF area of interest concerns the Australian Security Assistance Program, which is provided on a cash basis through foreign military sales (FMS). Among the many countries in the US Pacific Command area, Australia ranked first in total FMS purchases from fiscal years 1950 to 1986, with more than $US 6.2 billion spent. In 1986 alone Australia had 134 active Air Force-managed FMS cases, valued at more than $700 million in US currency.

Present USAF/Royal New Zealand Air Force (RNZAF) relations are about as good as they can be under the circumstances. Although USAF aircraft and aircrews are no longer involved in training and exercising with the RNZAF, more than 160 Air Force aircraft transited through New Zealand in 1986 (on their way to and from either Australia or Antarctica). Some 16 to 20 RNZAF aircraft transited through Hickam AFB, Hawaii, during the same time period. However, additional flying and landing restrictions are now in place. Effective April 1987 RNZAF aircraft were allowed access to US military airfields only under special circumstances, usually involving safety or security matters.[7]

Army

The US Army has its own approach in meeting objectives in the region. The land component wants and has involvement at various levels with the Australian Regular Army (ARA). They exercise often together. While the last military exercise the US Army had with the New Zealand Army was Triad 85, relations between army members from all three ANZUS countries continued at a reduced level.[8] The US Army's vehicle for achieving this continued contact is the Expanded Relations Program (ERP), run by Headquarters US Army Western Command, the US Army component of the US Pacific Command (USPACOM).

Established in 1978, the Expanded Relations Program was designed to implement USPACOM's peacetime strategy, complement its multinational strategy, enhance understanding and interoperability of the various military forces, improve selected nations' self-defense capabilities, and provide US Army Western Command forces with specialized training. The program consists of reciprocal visits, personnel exchanges, on-the-job training, combined command post and field training exercises, and a series of conferences and seminars. In recent years Headquarters Western Command has conducted, primarily through the ERP, military-to-military activities with 33 countries in the theater.

The centerpiece of the Expanded Relations Program was the Pacific Armies Management Seminar (PAMS). Conducted on a nonpolitical basis, the PAMS had a straightforward purpose—to "provide a forum for the discussion of common military management problems in a professional environment, to stimulate ideas, and to promote mutual understanding."[9] The growth of PAMS was impressive. Representatives from nine armies attended the first session in Honolulu in 1978. The 1986 session in Thailand had 196 representatives from 22 nations. Included in this gathering were senior officers from the New Zealand Army. As representatives of a friendly but not allied country, they actively interacted with members of the US Army. So PAMS, under the auspices of the ERP, affords at least a chance for US and New Zealand military professionals to keep in contact during the present period of strained political relations.[10]

The Asymmetry Factor

From the beginning of the formal alliance and its supporting relationships in the early 1950s, the United States was a willing participant in the asymmetrical relationship of seemingly unequal partners. Critical for the United States was the other two countries' acceptance of the role ANZUS had in preserving peace and freedom according to approved Western standards. This role had not only a regional context but also a critical linkage with the calculation of world peace, which depended on a stable nuclear deterrent. Such peace and freedom required national decisiveness and will to survive. From an American viewpoint, these fundamentals were all necessary parts of a modern Western security alliance and all partners needed to understand, accept, and adhere to them.[11]

The asymmetry factor was in reality a major part of the ANZUS relationship. Australia, with an urbanized population of 16.4 million, was a middle power in the world, comparable in many ways to Canada. New Zealand, with only 3.3 million citizens, was a small Western country with many of the characteristics of Denmark. These two neighbors were responsible for stability in their region of concern. (Appendix A lists the size and strength of their forces.) US policy was to share with Australia and New Zealand certain powers and privileges that were in excess of what those nations' smaller size and influence warranted. Both countries in turn were able to have considerable influence in dealing with the United States on a variety of security issues and other concerns. Active membership in ANZUS was a major reason for this favorable state of foreign affairs between the friendly Southwest Pacific nations and their North American ally.[12]

Australian Involvement

For Australia asymmetry in the former relationship did create some problems of perceived imbalance and irregularity of national intent and will. Australian officialdom occasionally had a tendency to assume that the special relationship between Australia and the United States was even greater than it really was. ANZUS helped perpetuate that thinking. To be sure, the United States needed Australia to host the joint facilities and provide port access to visiting US ships and their full complements of sailors and marines.

However, as Australia has gradually sought greater self-reliance and has become more concerned with its own defense needs, the strategic value of Australia to the United States has varied. In recent years political, economic, and societal factors caused these shifts as much as or more than military ones.[13] In the early 1970s strained relationships reflected frustration and dissatisfaction over involvement with the United States in the protracted Vietnam War. In the mid-1970s, at the start of the Liberal government of Prime Minister Malcolm Fraser, relations were generally good. In the late 1970s the relationship went slightly downward again, causing one of America's foremost experts on the region to comment on how the "ANZUS inheritance begins with a fairly obvious yet significant negative: the relative inconspicuousness of ANZUS for the United States."[14]

The truth was that Americans generally lacked knowledge and understanding of Australia's history, makeup, goals, and objectives. In recent years, however, an unofficial "special relationship and affinity" for the land and the people "down under," which many Americans have had for a long time, helped to strengthen Australian-American relationships.[15]

From a definite low point in the early 1970s, the United States for the most part has made official efforts to improve its relationship with Australia. For example, as the former US ambassador and the most senior career diplomat ever appointed to Australia, Marshall Green gave a highly publicized speech on Australian-American relations to the Asia Society of New York in 1975. In the speech he attempted to counter some of the ill feelings that had existed between Australian Labor Prime Minister Gough Whitlam and US President Richard Nixon.

> Perhaps the most important factor in our new relationship is Australia's insistence on doing its "own thing" in world affairs and our full acceptance of that fact.
>
> Over the past two years (1973-75), we have made it clear again and again that we do not look for a lock-step relationship. Such a rigid relationship could only snap in the winds of controversy. Today our relationship is flexible, based on mutuality and true equality.[16]

Much of Green's thinking appeared to be present again in the policies and practices of the Reagan administration concerning Australia and security in the region.

Admitting that ANZUS did provide definite security advantages for Australia and New Zealand, some Australian scholars still placed important negative qualifications on the relationship. First, the alliance seriously distorted Australian defense planning. Many deficiencies in recent defense posture and force structure stemmed directly from past requirements of ANZUS collective security. Questions rose about the defense forces' need for expensive high-technology weapons that required interoperability with US forces and systems. Whether access to highly sophisticated sources that provide raw and finished intelligence was really important to the defense of Australia was another area of discussion.[17] The Australian government attempted to address these and other points during a period of extensive review and debate in the 1980s.

When viewed as a showcase alliance in a no-problem region (despite negative and qualifying comments like those above), ANZUS was still useful to the involved countries. From an Australian perspective, ANZUS was an alliance between a medium power and a superpower which blended Australian politics and security into an effective arrangement with those of the United States. From an unofficial New Zealand perspective, compared to all realistic alternatives, ANZUS brought the most security for the country at the least cost.[18]

For more than 30 years, important senior-level officials used the annual ANZUS Council meetings as executive consultative forums. In settings that rotated among the three national capitals, the meetings covered a wide range of defense and foreign policy issues. The council meeting usually constituted the most important fixed item on the annual diplomatic calendar for both the Australian and New Zealand foreign ministers.[19] The three governments, acting through their foreign ministers and in turn their defense ministers, wanted to keep the Southwest Pacific region "Lake ANZUS." By pursuing this policy the ANZUS partners felt they were playing integral and legitimate roles in the global Western security network. Respective government-appointed representatives at the annual high-level meetings continually stressed the notion of deterrence in the alliance. The capabilities of the United States for nuclear deterrence and the relative capabilities of the United States, Australia, and New Zealand for collective conventional deterrence adequately provided the military components of the successful and seemingly durable ANZUS alliance.

Problems with New Zealand

Owing to the alliance's importance to regional and global security, the United States took a long time to negotiate with New Zealand the recent antinuclear issues that threatened the alliance. Through Wolfowitz, during the public and behind-the-scenes negotiations that started in 1984, the United States made a number of points very clear.

- The United States was proalliance and not pronuclear.
- The US government was fully aware of the long-standing nonnuclear policy of the New Zealand Labour Party, both in and out of government.
- The United States knew that there was little nuclear threat in the South Pacific region. Washington believed that all three ANZUS countries had a common interest in keeping strong and effective Western defense capabilities, primarily naval, in the region.
- The United States had only one navy, and it was nuclear.

- The United States followed a policy of neither confirm nor deny concerning questions of nuclear weapons on its ships and aircraft.

- New Zealand's "example" did not lead to mutual arms control but the opposite. By its actions New Zealand was curtailing its operational role—in effect, its cooperation and burden sharing—in the alliance.

The American reaction to New Zealand's antinuclear position and naval ship-banning policy was swift and decisive. As long as the reaction and ship ban policy continued, ANZUS was declared inoperative as a tripartite alliance. To demonstrate this to New Zealand and the rest of the watching Western world, the United States in 1985 and 1986 introduced several serious "punitive" measures. The superpower cut off New Zealand's access to high-grade intelligence, canceled all military exercises involving joint participation of American and New Zealand forces (highly valued by the small but professional New Zealand military), postponed indefinitely the annual ANZUS Council meeting, and finally, "closed" the long-standing and valuable "open door" policy between officials at various levels of the two governments. Within a short span of a few months in the mid-1980s, the ANZUS alliance had reached a crossroads of its usefulness and existence.[20] Although not canceling ANZUS per se, the US moves created a stronger bilateral security relationship with Australia and ended its security relationship with New Zealand. The United States no longer considered New Zealand to be the close ally it once was but just a friend.

Alliance Background
(1951-83: The First Three Decades)

To understand properly the present problems in ANZUS, one must also know about the beginnings and evolution of the alliance. What began as a simple collective security arrangement grew into a complex and wide-ranging one.

Until World War II, Australia and New Zealand (ANZ) were not in close alignment with the United States; instead they were fully integrated parts of the British imperial system. The 1941-43 Japanese advances suddenly revealed to Allied leaders the vital strategic importance of Australia and New Zealand to Pacific security. The circumstances of US entry into the war initially focused the attention of many Americans on Australian-New Zealand, and especially Australian, security. In 1942 Australia was the only base from which an effective Allied Pacific counteroffensive could be mounted against Japan. The British were no longer the major influence, the Americans were on the scene, and Australia and New Zealand were making their own important military contributions to the war effort. By 1944 the clear focus of an ANZ secure base faded, and US attention shifted northward to the clearing of the Central Pacific strategic sea lines of communication. Still, the total war experience changed forever the prewar stereotypes Australia and New Zealand had of the United States. Before, the United States was distant, somewhat unfamiliar, and of secondary importance. Great Britain was king. However, by the mid-to-late 1940s, like it or not, the United States was clearly the powerful bulwark upon which future ANZ security depended.[21]

The Australian basis of foreign policy was thus arguably "loyalty to a protector," at least until recent times. William F. Mandle, one writer of the period, suggests that Australian history "is not simply that of depending on a great and powerful friend, first Britain and then America, but of almost excruciating loyalty to its policies." [22] Sir Percy Spender, the conservative Australian minister for external affairs from 1949 to 1951 (and ambassador to the United States from 1951 to 1958) raised in the late 1940s the question of a viable Pacific defense pact. Fear of the United States setting up a "beneficent" peace with a possibly rearmed Japan caused Sir Percy to pursue with the Americans an assertive negotiating process on Pacific security. The US government principals involved were Secretaries of State Dean Acheson and John Foster Dulles of the Truman and Eisenhower administrations, respectively, and Assistant Secretary of State for East Asia Dean Rusk, who later was secretary of state in the Kennedy and Johnson administrations. None were overly enthusiastic in forming a Pacific security alliance.[23]

New Zealand's foreign policy in the postwar years was different from Australia's. More closely aligned with Great Britain, New Zealand was at a loss to fill the void left by the mother country's "security" withdrawal from the Pacific. Realities during and after the war brought a growing realization that Britain could no longer protect New Zealand security interests. This awareness led New Zealand for the first time in its history to seek a closer relationship with the United States. The "only one option apparently open" was taken with uneasiness.[24] Consequently, the beginning of the ANZUS alliance had an unusual trio of players. The new partners consisted of an unenthusiastic and begrudging superpower, the United States; an overanxious and accommodating middle power, Australia; and an uneasy and reluctant small power, New Zealand.

Formation Stage (1951-52)

ANZUS became an official treaty in the early 1950s. (See appendix B, The ANZUS Treaty.) Its formation stage covered the period from 1951 to 1952. The alliance took effect when signed into existence on 1 September 1951 in San Francisco by Sir Percy C. Spender for Australia, C. A. Berendsen for New Zealand, and Dean Acheson and John Foster Dulles for the United States. Sir Percy finally got his wish. A foundation now existed for a Western defensive pact in his region of strategic interest.[25]

By the time of its signing, the United States did in fact favor such a security agreement with former allies more than it had during the initial negotiations. One compelling reason for this change of official attitude was the growing American commitment to the idea that aggressive communism should be contained and resisted. The outbreak of the Korean War in June 1950 confirmed in the minds of many that offensive Communist expansion was again on the move. By chance several Australian air and naval units were in the North Pacific area at the time South Korea was invaded. The United States, first in the field as a United Nations agent in resisting these hostile advances, requested and obtained

Australian military support. Australia's readiness to assist the United States helped smooth the way to the ANZUS Treaty signing. The whole episode of ANZUS formation, Communist containment, the Japanese peace treaty, and the Korean War onset considerably readjusted the nature of the Australian-American relationship at the time. New Zealand more or less found itself supporting the two larger allies.[26]

Another agreement formed then by the ANZUS partners was the Radford-Collins agreement (named for Adm Arthur Radford, then commander in chief, Pacific Command, and VAdm Sir John Collins, the Australian chief of naval staff). It provided for the American, Australian, and New Zealand naval forces to share responsibility for protecting shipping and sea lines of communication in the strategically important South Pacific/Eastern Indian Ocean areas. Since its inception, the agreement has allowed the holding of joint operational exercises to improve their maritime protection, sea control, and antisubmarine warfare (ASW) capabilities. Since any future conflict of size and duration involving the ANZUS countries would include threats to shipping, Radford-Collins has continued to have relevance for merchant shipping protection in the region. Valid concerns include: merchant ship vulnerabilities, US Navy finite resources, vast maritime expanses, ANZ economies' dependence on international seaborne trade, and historical precedents of antishipping operations in the region during both world wars. When combined, the concerns assume greater significance and strengthen the need for Radford-Collins.[27]

Interim Stage (1953-75)

The interim stage, lasting more than 20 years from 1953 to 1975, saw the alliance grow into a solid and reasonably successful arrangement. By the end of the interim stage, however, major shifts of attitude and approach were present.

At first increasing interdependence and reliance upon the United States became important factors in Australian and New Zealand defense policies. The global collective security practices of the United States demanded an objective of "forward defense" when possible. To achieve this end for itself and its allies, the United States expected Australia and

New Zealand to contribute their fair share of support.[28] That meant continuing their program of providing forces for overseas deployment with a great ally. Since Australia and New Zealand no longer received any protection from Britain, they had to rely upon assistance from the United States. Although the scale of their overseas military contributions remained small, the political value that Australia and New Zealand gave to America was considerably greater. This support was most evident during their involvement in the Vietnam War of the 1960s and the early 1970s.

The establishment of joint US-Australian defense facilities on ANZ territory symbolized to many what ANZUS really was all about. The United States believed its two ANZUS partners had ideal locations for selected overseas defense establishments. Australia was especially appealing because of its strategic geographic location, remote areas, and stable political climate. By 1955 government officials signed an agreement for the first permanent joint installation in Australia. It was a seismic station whose purpose included gathering information on explosions, locating earthquakes, and undertaking research on earth physics.

This early arrangement led to a series of discussions and negotiations resulting in the establishment of many joint US-Australian defense facilities. The three largest and most important were Pine Gap, Nurrungar, and North West Cape. To varying degrees the bases became important aspects of American security and international military operations. The best-known facility was the Joint Defense Space Research Facility at Pine Gap, about 10 miles outside of Alice Springs in the center of Australia. Pine Gap had two functions, communication with satellites and development of strategic space technology. The facility staff numbered about 450, evenly divided between Americans and Australians.[29]

The Australian Labor government approved in 1988 another 10-year agreement for operation. Prime Minister Bob Hawke, representing the right wing of the Australian Labor Party (ALP), told officials in Washington that he accepted the risks of facilities like Pine Gap in view of "global strategic considerations."[30] Even former Prime Minister Gough Whitlam, aligned with the moderate wing of the ALP and at odds with official US policies, had cooperated. Though announcing in 1972 that he would make known to the public the functions of Pine Gap, he said after visits and briefings that Pine Gap was too vital and significant to reveal all of its operations. The Australian people were generally not upset then or later with these positions. A 1981 poll on the presence of the joint facilities showed 60 percent supported and only 22 percent opposed their presence.

The second important US-Australian facility was the Joint Defense Space Communications Station located at Nurrungar near Woomera in South Australia. Nurrungar was a principal fixed ground station for American military satellite communication in the Southern Hemisphere. Recently questions have arisen on whether fully operational satellite relay systems and mobile ground terminals would lessen the "strategic necessity" argument for Nurrungar. The consensus had the United States wishing to keep the facility to maintain redundancy.

The third important facility was the Harold E. Holt Naval Communications Station located at North West Cape, Western Australia. It provided secure communications for ships at sea.

Facilities like Pine Gap and Nurrungar, for reasons of geographic location, could only be placed in Australia. (See accompanying map.) North West Cape, however, could have its mission performed elsewhere.[31] These facilities have fluctuated in value and criticality over the years. The point to remember is that America believed that the joint facilities remained important and Australia felt that hosting them was a significant part of its contribution to ANZUS and to the deterrence of nuclear war.[32]

No joint US-New Zealand defense facilities existed on the latter's territory. Two American installations were in place. The first was the US Navy base near Christchurch at Harewood, South Island. For years the facility provided primary allied support for Operation Deep Freeze to Antarctica. The second installation was an American astronomical observatory in the Black Birch range, also on the South Island. Although these facilities were not so critical as the joint facilities in Australia, the United States still valued them. It was thus a matter of concern when, for political reasons, Secretary of the US Navy John Lehman talked

Australia

Source: *Australia Background Notes* (Washington, D.C.: Department of State, Bureau of Public Affairs, August 1986), 2.

unofficially about moving his service's fairly extensive facility from Christchurch to Hobart, Tasmania, situated off the southeastern coast of mainland Australia.

ANZUS development encompassed a great deal more than just security matters. It covered a wide range of programs, including intelligence-maritime surveillance support, logistics and supply support, trilateral conferences, consultations, defense cooperation, and more. Although these programs were often erroneously referred to as part of ANZUS, they officially were not because other directives and agreements governed them. However, the ANZUS Treaty provided a suitable facilitating mechanism to make the varied processes function smoothly and efficiently.[33]

While the interim years saw the establishment of many ANZUS features, they also marked the beginnings of opposition to the alliance in Australia and New Zealand. The Vietnam War caused initial discontent and protests. Almost three years before ANZ combat troops were committed to Vietnam in 1965, supposedly at the request of the United States, there was a small Australian military presence there comprised of volunteer regular ground forces but no draftees. In 1964 the Australian government reintroduced conscription by using a lottery system that made nonvolunteers eligible to serve overseas. Once conscripts started to go to Vietnam in 1966, the issues of the "lottery of death" came to overshadow almost all other factors in the public debate on Australia's role and involvement in Vietnam.[34]

Synonymous with this was the brief "lock-step" relationship which then Prime Minister Harold E. Holt exercised with President Lyndon B. Johnson. Holt was the man who proclaimed that Australia was "all the way with LBJ" concerning Vietnam. It was a rare instance in which Australia mounted a peacetime military effort commensurate with its population and economic resources. The attitude was short-lived and reached a turning point with Johnson's dramatic 1968 policy reversal in Vietnam and withdrawal from the presidential elections. That moment marked a real crisis not just in, but of, the Australian-American alliance.[35]

Antinuclear attitudes were also beginning to surface during this time. In conjunction with growing opposition in the late 1960s to ANZ involvement with the United States in Vietnam, questions began to rise as to the value of the alliance and the complicated issue of nuclear weapons. In the early 1970s the New Zealand Labour Party (NZLP), especially under the leadership of Norman Kirk and Sir Wallace Rowling (later New Zealand's ambassador to the United States), advocated a nuclear free zone in the South Pacific. During the same period, the Australian Labor Party, led by Gough Whitlam, also had significant views that clashed with Washington's perceptions of strategic interests. Organized protests became more common in the years surrounding the pullout of ANZ military forces from Vietnam in 1972 and during the concurrent terms of the two labor governments. While still supportive of ANZUS, the public was upset with the general direction of events. These antinuclear attitudes were temporarily shelved by the mid-1970s elections of conservative governments pledged to defense support and close alliance ties with the United States. Yet many negative sentiments did not disappear but only remained in the background.[36]

Two more shocks disrupted the ANZ perception of American security and alliance support. First was President Nixon's 1969 announcement in Guam stressing that from then on the United States could not be expected to come to everyone's defense and that basically each country needed to defend itself. From an Australian point of view, this meant that "forward defense" was no longer viable and that its foreign policy of securing the region by means of great power commitments was over. If the United States, like Great Britain before, was leaving the region, Australia had to develop a greater degree of self-reliance in defense policy. To counter these concerns American officials stressed that the Nixon Doctrine was grossly distorted when applied thus to ANZUS and NATO. It applied primarily to friends and allies in Asia and provided a way for American extrication from Vietnam. While Australia and New Zealand were listening to this argument, the second shock came. This was the fall of Saigon in 1975 and the subsequent end of US combat presence in Southeast Asia.[37]

Later Stage (1976-83)

The later alliance stage covered 1976 to 1983. Conservative governments came into power in the mid-1970s: Malcolm Fraser's Liberal Party in Australia and Robert Muldoon's National Party in New Zealand. In white papers on defense (Australia in 1976 and New Zealand in 1978 and 1983), both governments pushed for greater efforts for self-reliant defense forces. Yet, in Australia especially, their attempts to devise new, credible, and self-reliant policies led in many respects back to the need for continued close military, technical, and intelligence ties with the United States.

Increasing inflationary and other economic problems began to impose restrictions upon the relatively modest defense spending of both Australia and New Zealand. Although initially enthusiastic about substantial increases for defense, the Fraser government had trouble devoting more than 2.5 percent of the gross domestic product (GDP—the national income) to it. New Zealand's very modest defense establishment used only about 1.8 percent of its GDP for defense. When adjusted to the country's population and resources, this was one of the world's lowest figures.

By the mid-1980s two opposing viewpoints concerning ANZUS alliance management began to emerge. The American position was fairly consistent and advocated no drastically new approaches to collective security. It stressed burden-sharing responsibilities within a successful defense alliance. Each active partner needed to make expected and reasonable contributions. For the alliance to be effective and worthwhile, a spirit of cooperation that involved military, political, and economic aspects had to prevail.[38]

Antipodean positions differed from American ones at times. Active support or defense by the United States was no longer a guarantee. To some, provisions in the ANZUS Treaty were not binding. The region, especially in the South Pacific, was a no-threat environment. The ANZUS nuclear umbrella reportedly caused some installations in Australia and New Zealand—particularly the joint defense facilities in Australia—to become targets on a Soviet nuclear hit list. Public officials emphasized that nuclear arms control commitments had priority over alliance commitments. As a result both Australia and New Zealand recognized an increasing need for more self-reliance in defense and greater regional considerations for security stability.[39]

Current Conditions (1984 to Present)

The ANZUS alliance reached a point of disarray in the mid-1980s. While such a low point was never the expressed goal of national leaders on any side, some observers have called for changes in policy and emphasis. Since much of the disagreement now centered on fundamental issues, the current crisis could not be viewed as light or temporary.

Australian Support

Significant political changes came with the election of Labor Party governments in Australia in 1983 and in New Zealand in 1984. Many believed that the Australian Labor Party, headed by the charismatic Bob Hawke, would take the lead in changing Australian relations with the United States concerning ANZUS and many other bilateral agreements. Yet Hawke and his government surprised most observers by attempting to improve upon the already strong ties with the United States. The most obvious example of this approach was the comprehensive review of the entire ANZUS arrangement the ALP conducted immediately after entering office. The new government concluded that the treaty supported Australian security in current and prospective strategic circumstances. Hawke clearly stated that, "we will maintain Australia's commitment to the ANZUS Treaty. . . . The ANZUS alliance will not only be adhered to by my Government, but it will be strengthened in the sense of frank discussions with the US about whether in any way it may be improved."[40]

New Zealand Turning Point

If the ALP's position on ANZUS gave the United States a slight degree of comfort, the New Zealand Labour Party's stance the following year certainly did not. The 1984 election of 43-year-old David Lange as New Zealand's youngest prime minister represented a turning point, although not a new one, in New Zealand's approach to foreign and defense policies. Lange inherited a well-supported NZLP government policy that contained two essential elements. The first, seemingly contradictory, denied entry to New Zealand ports of foreign warships (primarily American, but also others, including the British) that were nuclear powered, nuclear armed, or, in light of the official US neither-confirm-nor-deny stance, nuclear capable. Yet, at the same time, the policy wanted New Zealand to remain an active member of ANZUS and continue to participate in joint military exercises with the other two member countries. The second element called for a nuclear weapons free environment established throughout the South Pacific maritime region—the South Pacific Nuclear Free Zone, or SPNFZ. As far as New Zealand officials were concerned, ANZUS was a conventional defensive alliance. Ambassador Rowling, the former NZLP leader who initially helped propose these positions, wrote, "New Zealand has never formed part of a nuclear strategy. We have not asked nor do we expect to be defended by nuclear weapons. From our perspective, ANZUS has always been a conventional defence relationship." [41]

Port access quickly became a nonnegotiable issue for both sides and culminated in the banning of the USS *Buchanan* in February 1985. To state their government's position, American officials, along with those from Australia and the outgoing New Zealand conservative government, released a communiqué shortly after Lange's election saying it was essential that allied warships continue to have access to New Zealand facilities just as they had in the past. During the five-year period from 1980 to 1984, almost 40 US naval vessels, at least six of which were nuclear powered, had called on New Zealand ports.

New Zealand's leaders countered by stating they resented the implication that their only contribution to ANZUS was provision of port facilities for US Navy ships. Supporting their point was the fact that only four American ships visited in 1981 and two in 1982, during a time the United States said such port visits were vital. From the New Zealand perspective, that was a "pretty thin relationship." [42] The impasse on the port access began to dominate and cloud all other discussions.

Two points stood out regarding the dispute. First, the ANZUS difficulties underscored the need for greater American alertness to allies' domestic political trends before an impasse point was reached. Second, the United States (and other Western nations) overlooked the fact that New Zealand had been making important contributions to South Pacific stability and development for decades and that its closeness to Polynesia was unmatched.[43]

If Prime Minister Lange did not totally believe in the NZLP position before his election, he quickly became a convert and strong advocate of his small country's determined stance to speak out on nuclear weapons and the escalating arms race between the superpowers. For months after the election, the international news media and the public paid an inordinate amount of attention to the young leader and his quest for nuclear weapons "sanity." He was even nominated for the Nobel Peace Prize. Although he did not win the peace prize, Lange was still able to present his case to the world.

Regardless of future New Zealand security policies, Lange spoke of the following imperatives he planned to push for. He wanted:

- to provide for the conventional defense of New Zealand (most important obligation);
- to contribute toward South Pacific security in all its aspects;
- to promote economic interests of New Zealand;
- to pay regard to defense arrangements of its closest and most important partner, Australia; and
- to take into account the attitude of the United States toward New Zealand when thinking about the security relationship.

The New Zealand prime minister highlighted several other fundamental points in the dispute. In their rejection of the ship visits, New Zealanders were not anti-American, only antinuclear. They were offended by comments that they were not pulling their weight in the alliance. As far as New Zealand was concerned, they knew much about proper burden sharing. New Zealand did not offer itself as an example for others to follow. Its strategic circumstances were unique. The government excluded nuclear weapons and power because having them there was not in the country's interests. While the United States saw ANZUS in the context of its global East-West strategy of nuclear deterrence, New Zealand viewed its own role and common interest to be that of a regional conventional deterrent promoting international security. If the United States continued to insist upon having nuclear weapons in the region, then maybe that was too high a price for New Zealand to pay. The final main point Lange and others wanted to make with the United States was that by punishing and disengaging itself from New Zealand on defense issues, the superpower was going to lose a loyal ally and a true friend.[44]

United States Response

The US response was predictably one of measured frustration. New Zealand's actions were a "matter of grave concern, which goes to the core of our mutual obligation of allies."[45] The United States worried that neutralist or isolationist thinking was beginning to enter several realms of allied foreign policy. Evidence that this was happening was the Lange government's nonnegotiable no-nuclear-weapons policy asserted in "tones of moral righteousness."[46] Paul Wolfowitz perhaps best explained the Department of State's position and subsequent actions at a 1985 symposium on Pacific security.

> For an ally to insist on that kind of disclosure [NCND] as a condition for port access is just not responsible. . . .

> With words, New Zealand assures us it remains committed to ANZUS. But by its deeds, New Zealand has effectively curtailed its operational role in the alliance. . . . A military alliance has little meaning without military cooperation. . . . New Zealand can't have it both ways.[47]

Regardless of the number of vessels that actually visited, the ship ban, according to American officials, put the US Navy at a considerable disadvantage and weakened its ability to help the ANZUS partners. The Navy saw negative effects spreading throughout the various Pacific maritime areas. Adm Ronald Hays, commander in chief of the US Pacific Command, spoke of "the US having lost New Zealand when it formally passed [antinuclear ship ban] legislation." The United States was being forced to take "appropriate measures" to show that such action was not acceptable conduct by an ally. To indicate the seriousness of the banning issue, the United States ended in 1986 a two-year period of negotiations and considerable effort with New Zealand by "parting company . . . as friends." [48]

Several side effects resulted from the ANZUS controversy. One was the perception that the United States was being an inflexible superpower trying to impose its will on the smaller members of a Western security arrangement. Another was the volatile issue of economic trade restrictions. This was most readily apparent when raised as a major agenda item at the bilateral American-Australian security meeting held in San Francisco in August 1986. The cause for concern was the unexpected severity of the Australian backlash against the American government due to its offer to subsidize export wheat sales from the United States to the Soviet Union. Although the Australian government resisted pressures to link "unfair" US trade practices and joint defense facilities, the Australian public did not. For the first time, many Australian citizens interlocked the separate issues and questioned the value of the American-Australian defense alliance relationship. Australians found it ironic that while loyalty to the United States in the ANZUS antinuclear dispute was reportedly causing their country to lose a potential $A 700-900 million in export earnings, American-New Zealand trade increased marginally during the same period. The most unusual Australian political combination of the traditionally conservative rural farmers and the radical leftist urban and trade union groups was very critical of American trade policies for a while. Even though the furor over trade issues and alliance linkage subsided, it was indicative of still unresolved problems, which might have explained Prime Minister Hawke's comment that in many respects ANZUS had become by the mid-1980s a "treaty in name only." [49]

Future Status

The future of ANZUS as a trilateral defense alliance is unknown. Fundamental questions that still require answers are many. How can the situation be salvaged and the damage limited? Where does New Zealand go from here? How strong will the bilateral defense relationships be that exist between Australia and the United States and between Australia and New Zealand? Can and should Australia assume a middle-partner bridging role? Will ANZUS ever return to the way it was? Was the Western security arrangement for the region impaired by all these disturbances? Few easy answers exist for these and other questions. If satisfactory answers had been available, negotiations would have been successful and grievances on all sides would have been redressed, and discussion of the 35-year-old showcase alliance being in crisis and at a major crossroads of its existence would not be ongoing. The best way to think about the ANZUS alliance status in the years ahead is to discuss some of the major factors that will influence events and policies.

United States Position

The official US position on alliance goals and responsibilities is clear and uncompromising. Secretary of State George P. Shultz expressly stated that the purpose of defense alliances will continue to be to deter aggression and preserve peace by making it clear that allied nations will unite to oppose aggressors. The real deterrent will continue to be allies working together to ensure that capabilities exist to fight and win conflicts. The supporting part of the deterrent will be that any potential aggressor will know it. According to Shultz, ANZUS as an alliance is not finished. It remains fully operational between the United States and Australia today. With some adjustments by New Zealand, the United States will welcome the former partner's full participation in the treaty again. While it does not expect New Zealand to endorse a strategic nuclear policy, the United States expects New Zealand to do its fair share in maintaining stability and deterrence in the region. For the Americans this includes unqualified access of their ships to New Zealand ports. The issue is not one of numbers or type. The demonstrative effect of New Zealand acceptance and participation is important for a fully functioning ANZUS. When New Zealand policies and actions change accordingly, the United States will restore its security arrangements with New Zealand to include joint exercises, intelligence information sharing, logistics supply, and support. Each of the allies, America included, will then need greater regional security roles.[50]

New Zealand Posture

New Zealand, at least as long as the Lange Labour government was in control, remained unwilling to negotiate its position on nuclear weapons. It did not accept the American view of what New Zealand obligations should be under ANZUS. Its policies were for New Zealand only, and the country's stance was antinuclear and not anti-American. The small country did not think that its policies justified the actions the United States was taking against it. According to Bryce Harland, the former New Zealand permanent representative to the United Nations and then high commissioner in London, there were several key points to remember about his country's policies. New Zealand, isolated and remote, did not set its policy as an example to any other country. In fact, no other member of the Western alliance was following New Zealand's actions. Its case was unique and not relevant to others. American reactions worried other small countries and had possibly more negative effects on the alliance than New Zealand's own actions. New Zealand was taking steps to compensate for the US suspension of military cooperation. What remained unknown was the long-term ability of New Zealand's own small armed forces to contribute to the security of the region outside of an ANZUS structure.[51]

Australian Perspective

Australia's perspective was more positive. It felt its bilateral relations with the United States had increased and thus had improved its position and status not only with America but also with the other countries in the region. The Australian public, despite some trade issue dissatisfaction, still overwhelmingly supported ANZUS. In 1985, 73 percent agreed that Australia needed a defense alliance with the United States. If New Zealand were no longer in ANZUS, an even greater total of 75 percent favored a separate mutual defense alliance with the United States. Security cooperation remained close, and it was difficult to see this situation changing significantly in the near future. When all factors were considered, Australia would attempt to fulfill its regional security obligations under ANZUS. An unknown factor was a growing and potent antinuclear element in its own country. As yet that faction did not appear to be as strong as similar ones in New Zealand and elsewhere in the areas covered by the proposed South Pacific Nuclear Free Zone.

Summary

The basic ANZUS alliance and the many security and defense arrangements that resulted from it directly or indirectly have undergone many shifts during the treaty's existence. Although ANZUS was thought to be a showcase alliance in a low-threat part of the world, recent events have shown it to be in trouble. Part of the problem may be the imbalance caused by the special asymmetrical relationship between three similar but different partners. Perhaps the national security objectives and political aspirations of each were in fact far enough apart to mean ANZUS could no longer continue as it had in the past. The split between the United States and New Zealand over the nuclear ship ban issue reflected some long-standing beliefs that reached a crisis point in the mid-1980s. Australia, which stood to benefit in some ways from the dispute, also found itself caught in the middle and was disturbed by overall developments.

To be effective any defense alliance must be at least a two-way street. If a member does not pull a fair load, then that member may be more hindrance than help. In this case, new arrangements are at least conceivable, if not essential. The viability, indeed the survivability, of ANZUS as an alliance is not inevitable. National self-interest alone can never replace common interest and a spirit of cooperation as fundamental components of an alliance like ANZUS.[52]

Along with the former solid alliance being at a crossroads of at least its usefulness, if not its existence, other recent and projected changes under way in the Southwest Pacific promise to reshape the way Western collective security is provided to the vast region. Both Australia and

New Zealand are rethinking the roles, missions, and structures of their conventional defense forces. One result has been a marked variation in the way these forces relate to their long-time partner, the United States, to include the military, government, and industrial sectors. Each of the smaller countries has a stated goal to be more independent, self-reliant, and realistic with its defense features, whether within or without a revised ANZUS framework. The altering defense features of Australia and New Zealand require detailed examination to determine their origins, directions headed, and means planned to see them through. The first ANZUS partner to be reviewed is Australia—a key Western security link to the South Pacific, Southeast Asia, and the Indian Ocean.

Notes

1. Quoted in Dora Alves, *The ANZUS Partners*, Georgetown University Significant Issue Series 6, no. 8 (Washington, D.C.: Center for Strategic and International Studies, 1984), appendix 1, 61; P. Lewis Young, "ANZUS: Politics of an Alliance," *Asian Defence Journal*, December 1982, 67.

2. Alves, 22; Owen Harries, "Crisis in the Pacific," *Commentary*, June 1985, 50-51.

3. Paul D. Wolfowitz, "The ANZUS Alliance," *Current Policy*, no. 674 (18 March 1985): 1.

4. Paul D. Wolfowitz, "The ANZUS Relationship: Alliance Management," *Current Policy*, no. 592 (24 June 1984): 4-5.

5. Confidential discussions with Headquarters US Pacific Command and Headquarters US Pacific Fleet military officials at Camp Smith and Pearl Harbor Naval Station, Hawaii, March 1987; US Department of State, telegram, subject: Secretary's Statements at San Francisco, 152332Z August 1986, 1.

6. "USAF-RAAF Airman-to-Airman Talks," (U), Headquarters US Air Force, Deputy Chief of Staff, Plans, issue paper, 16 October 1986, 1-2. Information extracted is unclassified.

7. Confidential discussions with Headquarters US Pacific Air Forces (USPACAF) and Headquarters Strategic Air Command military officials at Hickam AFB, Hawaii, March 1987; "Australian Security Assistance Program," Headquarters PACAF Deputy Chief of Staff, Plans, background paper, Hickam AFB, Hawaii, 26 February 1987, 1.

8. Confidential discussions with Headquarters US Western Command military officials at Fort Shafter, Hawaii, March 1987.

9. "WESTCOM Expanded Relations Program," Headquarters US Western Command, information paper, Fort Shafter, Hawaii, 19 February 1987, 1.

10. Ibid.

11. Wolfowitz, "The ANZUS Relationship," 3.

12. Robert A. Brand, "Defence Down Under: An American View," *Pacific Defence Reporter* 11, no. 12 (June 1985): 12.

13. Fedor A. Mediansky, "United States Interests in Australia," *Australian Outlook* 30, no. 1 (April 1976): 153-54.

14. Henry S. Albinski, "American Perspectives on the ANZUS Alliance," *Australian Outlook* 32, no. 2 (August 1978): 131.

15. Henry S. Albinski, *ANZUS: The United States and Pacific Security* (Lanham, Md.: University Press of America, 1987), 11; Joseph M. Siracusa, "Further Reflections on United States Interests in Australia," *Australian Outlook* 30, no. 3 (December 1976): 475, 479.

16. Siracusa, 476.

17. Fedor A. Mediansky, "Australia's Security and the American Alliance," *Australian Outlook*, April 1983, 24.

18. P. Lewis Young, 67; Ramesh Thakur, "New Zealand and ANZUS: From Milestone to Millstone?" *Asian Defence Journal*, December 1984, 17.

19. Harries, 49.

20. Ibid.; Wolfowitz, "The ANZUS Alliance," 1-3; Dora Alves, *Anti-nuclear Attitudes in New Zealand and Australia* (Washington, D.C.: National Defense University Press, 1985), 61; Secretary's Statements at San Francisco, 1.

21. J. G. Starke, *The ANZUS Treaty Alliance* (Melbourne, Australia: Melbourne University Press, 1965), 4; Glen St. John Barclay, "The Future of Australian-American Relations," *Australian Outlook* 30, no. 3 (December 1976): 466, 470; Robert A. Brand, "Australia, New Zealand, and ANZUS," *Atlantic Community Quarterly* 22, no. 4 (Winter 1984-85): 346-47; idem, "Defense Down Under," 11.

22. William F. Mandle, *Going It Alone: Australia's National Identity in the Twentieth Century* (Melbourne, Australia: The Penguin Press, 1977), 128.

23. Sir Percy C. Spender, *Exercises in Diplomacy: The ANZUS Treaty and the Columbo Plan* (New York: New York University Press, 1969), 13, 63.

24. Albinski, "American Perspectives," 131-32; David Lange, "New Interests, New Paths," *New Zealand Foreign Affairs Review* 35, no. 2 (April-June 1985): 10-11.

25. *The ANZUS Treaty Alliance*, a list of signatories at San Francisco, September 1951, 6; quoted in Alves, *The ANZUS Partners*, appendix, 60-63.

26. Mandle, 134-35; Thomas-Durell Young, "United States Security Interests and Objectives" (paper presented at a seminar on Strategic Imperatives and Western Responses in the South and Southwest Pacific, Sydney, Australia, 9-12 February 1986), 46.

27. Thomas-Durell Young, "Don't Abandon Radford-Collins," *Pacific Defence Reporter* 13, no. 3 (September 1986): 16.

28. Organization of the Joint Chiefs of Staff, *United States Military Posture for FY 1987* (Washington, D.C.: Department of Defense, Summer 1986), 4-5.

29. Harry G. Gelber, "Australia, the United States and the Strategic Balance: Some Comments on the Joint Facilities," *Australian Outlook* 36, no. 2 (August 1982): 13.

30. Thomas Keneally, *Outback* (London: Rand McNally Publishing Co., 1983), 141; Derek McDougall, "The Hawke Government's Policies towards the USA," *Round Table*, no. 310 (April 1989): 169.

31. Gelber, 13; Thomas W. Shubert, "The United States and the Southwest Pacific: Policy Options for a Changing Region" (master's thesis, Naval Postgraduate School, March 1986), 35-36. Many Australian strategists, academics, and journalists have commented on the value and need for the joint facilities. See P. Lewis Young, 70; Denis Warner, "The Importance of Being ANZUS," *Pacific Defence Reporter* 11, no. 3 (September 1984): 21; Frank Robertson, "Pine Gap Raises Its Outer Veil," *Pacific Defence Reporter* 12, no. 10 (April 1986): 14; Mediansky, "United States Interests in Australia," 142, 153; John Stackhouse, "A Glimpse at a Growing Pine Gap," *The Bulletin* 108, no. 5507 (25 February 1986): 52; Keneally, 141; Andrew Mack, "U.S. Bases in Australia: The Controversy Grows," *Asian Defence Journal*, November 1984, 50-53.

32. Gerald L. Purcell, "The Value and Future of the ANZUS Alliance," *Journal of the Australian Naval Institute* 11, no. 1 (February 1985): 14; Anthony Bergin, "Asian Security in Australian Perspective," *Asian Defence Journal*, October 1985, 81-82; Fedor A. Mediansky, "ANZUS in Crisis," *Australian Quarterly* 57, nos. 1 and 2 (Autumn-Winter 1985): 15.

33. Thomas-Durell Young, "An Analysis of and Commentary on the Australian, New Zealand, and United States Defence Relationship, 1951-1986" (PhD diss., University of Geneva, 1987), 245-55, appendix E; Peter Samuel, "New Zealand Anti-Nuclear View Driving U.S. Naval Operations to Australia," *New York City Tribune*, 11 March 1987, 5.

34. Henry S. Albinski, *Politics and Foreign Policy in Australia: The Impact of Vietnam and Conscription* (Durham, N.C.: Duke University Press, 1970), 39; Mandle, 141.

35. Hugh Collins, "Australia and the United States: Assessing the Relationship," *Australian Outlook* 32, no. 2 (August 1978): 156.

36. Lange, "New Interests, New Paths," 11; Albinski, "American Perspectives," 135.

37. Gelber, 14; John C. Dorrance, "ANZUS: Misperceptions, Mythology and Reality," *Australian Quarterly* 57, no. 3 (Spring 1985): 218-19.

38. Dorrance, 222, 229; Gelber, 14-15; Albinski, "American Perspectives," 141-42; Tony Street, "Alliances, Threats and the World around Us: No 1—Why Australia Is Aligned," *Pacific Defence Reporter* 9, no. 8 (February 1983): 10.

39. Mediansky, "ANZUS in Crisis," 7-9, 17; Lange, "New Interests, New Paths," 11-12; Keneally, 141.

40. Bergin, 81; Brand, "Australia, New Zealand, and ANZUS," 349.

41. John H. Beaglehole, "No 1—New Zealand: The End of an Era," *Pacific Defence Reporter* 11, no. 10 (April 1985): 8; Shubert, 31; Peter Samuel and P. F. Serong, "The Troubled Waters of ANZUS," *Strategic Review* 14, no. 1 (Winter 1986): 42.

42. Allan C. Brownfeld, "Fragility of Alliance Illustrated in New Zealand," *Washington Times*, 12 September 1984, 3C-4C; Beaglehole, 8; Graham Ansell,

"ANZUS Stand Explained," *New Zealand Foreign Affairs Review* 35, no. 1 (January-March 1985): 48.

43. Dora Alves, "Strategic Imperatives to Strengthen the Fabric of Peace in the Pacific" (paper presented at a seminar on Strategic Imperatives and Western Responses in the Pacific, Sydney, Australia, 9-12 February 1986), 76.

44. David Lange, "Relations with the United States," *New Zealand Foreign Affairs Review* 35, no. 3 (July-September 1985): 31-32; idem, "Nuclear Policy Sparks Debate," *New Zealand Foreign Affairs Review* 35, no. 1 (January-March 1985): 5-7; idem, "New Interests, New Paths," 13; idem, "New Zealand's Security Policy," *Foreign Affairs* 63, no. 5 (Summer 1985): 1015.

45. Beaglehole, 10.

46. Samuel and Serong, 44-45.

47. Quoted in Denis Warner, "No 2—'New Zealand Can't Have It Both Ways,'" *Pacific Defence Reporter* 11, no. 10 (April 1985): 12; Alves, *Anti-nuclear Attitudes in New Zealand and Australia*, 61.

48. Brand, "Australia, New Zealand, and ANZUS," 357; Ronald J. Hays, "Soviet Shadow Is Apparent in Pacific Security Setting," *San Diego Union*, 10 August 1986, 6C; "U.S.-New Zealand Disagreement on Port Access for U.S. Ships," *Department of State Bulletin* 86, no. 2114 (September 1986): 87; Albinski, *ANZUS: The United States and Pacific Security*, 49-50.

49. Statement of James R. Lilley, US deputy assistant secretary of state for East Asia and Pacific Affairs, in House Committee on Foreign Affairs, *United States Policy toward New Zealand and Australia and the Current State of ANZUS: Hearings before the Subcommittee on Asian and Pacific Affairs*, 99th Cong., 2d sess., 25 September 1986, 8-9; Fedor A. Mediansky, "Washington Startled by a Roaring Mouse Down Under," *The Bulletin* 108, no. 5544 (11 November 1986): 118; Oakland Ross, "South Pacific Shakes Fist at the U.S.," *Toronto Globe & Mail*, 25 October 1986, 3D; Beaglehole, 11.

50. George P. Shultz, "On Alliance Responsibility," *Department of State Bulletin* 85, no. 2012 (September 1985): 33; Caspar W. Weinberger, "We Would Welcome New Zealand's Return Anytime," *Pacific Islands Monthly* 56, no. 12 (December 1985): 20.

51. Bryce Harland, "A Continuing Partnership," *New Zealand Foreign Affairs Review* 35, no. 2 (April-June 1985): 27-28; Brian L. Kavanagh, *The Changing Western Alliance in the South Pacific* (Maxwell AFB, Ala.: Air University Press, 1987), 20.

52. Ross Babbage, "The Prospects for Security Cooperation between ANZUS Allies till the Turn of the Century" (paper presented at the National Defense University Conference on the Pacific Basin Security: Impact of Political and Social Change toward Year 2000, Honolulu, Hawaii, 27 February 1987), 14-15; "Whither the Alliance?" *Air Force Times*, 9 February 1987, 28.

Chapter 3

Australian Defense Features

Australia regards its relationship with the United States as of fundamental importance. . . . We will be together forever.

—Bob Hawke, Prime Minister of Australia

We [plan to] shape [limited defence capabilities] primarily to defend Australia and Australian interests in very large areas which are our immediate defence environment.

—F. Rawdon Dalrymple, Australian Ambassador to the United States

The images of the Australian fighting man at war have often been those of rugged individualism, fierce courage, unswerving loyalty to his "mates," and staunch self-reliance. These representations have formed a large part of the myth and the national self-image that Australians and others, including Americans, have when thinking about the defense forces of the land "down under." The truth is that Australians at war generally have proved themselves well. Fighting under the British and then with the United States, they have shown through deeds their worthiness as valued comrades in arms.

In peacetime the Australian military forces have not always earned as many accolades from foreigners or even from their own countrymen. In the mid-1980s Minister of Defence Kim Beazley described the Australian Defence Force (ADF) as "capable, well-trained, well-equipped, and well-led."[1] At the same time defense critics considered the ADF to have "little bits of lots" of capabilities.[2] To help address this issue, Beazley commissioned a one-year in-depth study of the situation by Paul Dibb, a recognized authority on Australian policy and defense matters.

43

The resulting report, *Review of Australia's Defence Capabilities: Report to the Minister for Defence* (the Dibb report), published in 1986, was hailed as the most significant review of Australian defense capabilities, force structure, and related aspects since the Second World War. This report formed the basis for the 1987 government white paper on defense policy, considered by many to be a landmark document. Both the Dibb report and the white paper were important parts of the story of a country on the brink of a major restructuring of defense policy and military force structure. Australia was trying to address its shortcomings while remaining committed to policies and practices supporting allied interests and self-reliance.[3] Were these diverse objectives achievable? This chapter examines the multitude of issues involved with the changing Australian defense features. It considers Australia's current defense posture, then examines how it came about. For a chronological framework, it looks at two general settings: before and after 1986, the year of the Dibb report. Other areas are then discussed prior to a final section on the growing bilateral Australian and American defense relationship.

The Role of the Australian Defence Force

Australia, a Western country with fairly diverse economic and political structures, considers itself as a regional middle power within the Western global alliance system. With a mostly Caucasian population of 16.4 million, more than 70,500 people serve on active duty as volunteer members of the ADF. The reserve military is more than 26,000, mostly in the army, and the civilian force working full time in the Department of Defence exceeds 40,000.[4] Consequently, there are almost 137,000 (less than 1 percent of the population) Australians directly associated with some aspect of the peacetime defense force. The ADF strives to support a pro-Western and pro-ANZUS governmental policy that revolves around a high-technology, conventional military force. Although the Australian public until recently has not been particularly involved in public debate on defense issues, it has been supportive of both an effective and a capable ADF and the ANZUS arrangement. In 1984 *The Bulletin* magazine's special survey of Australians disclosed that:

- 74 percent favored increased defense spending;
- 62 percent favored compulsory military training for all young men
- (39 percent for young women);
- 57 percent believed some countries threatened Australia's security; and
- 68 percent believed its defense treaties with its close ally, the United States, were of great value to Australia.[5]

Yet manpower figures and public samplings did not answer all the questions needed for debate on the ADF and defense policy. A concerted effort for informed debate was required to determine whether Australia had the appropriate mix of a reasonably self-reliant defense capability and a certain degree of dependence on overseas support (primarily the United States) to meet its defense objectives. The Dibb report and the follow-on government white paper, *The Defence of Australia* 1987, were steps in the right direction for addressing the changing Australian defense features. Comments on earlier features of the ADF are necessary to put a discussion of an ANZUS chronology into proper context.

US-Australian Historical Defense Ties

In the past the United States has been a factor in Australian defense thinking as a means to help protect the country and its interests. According to some observers, the idea began in the late nineteenth century, and it was expressed in the White Australia policy that was a function of the newly federated country's fear of an industrious and formidable Japan. For this reason, Australia's Prime Minister Alfred Deakin in 1908 engineered a visit to Australia by US President Theodore Roosevelt's Great White Fleet. Deakin also tried but failed to see enunciated an American (and British) "Monroe Doctrine of the Pacific."

The Australian fear of the original Japanese threat dominated their political thinking for almost 40 years. The widespread belief that America saved Australia from the Japanese (and the Germans in the South Pacific) during the darkest days of World War II remained an important source for much of the lasting pro-US sentiment and high-level popular support for ANZUS. The idea of a special Monroe Doctrine has not gone away. Current Minister of Defence Beazley has spoken of an assertion of Australian regional leadership, with American backing, reflected in a modern Monroe Doctrine in the South Pacific. Beazley's comments were indicative of the general attitude about the necessary and continuing strong defense ties with America.[6]

Wartime Performance of Australian Forces

Despite close association with the American military during wartime, the ADF (and incidentally the New Zealand Defence Forces) accomplished and contributed enough to stand out on their own. The combined exploits of Australia and New Zealand (ANZ) in both world wars were well known. The military had a proven reputation and high standard of performance in battle. Their tradition based itself on maintaining top-quality volunteer forces capable of rapid movement in regional contingencies and on serving as the professional cadre of much larger defense forces in times of wider need.[7]

Considering its population base and other requirements, the efforts of the ADF in both global wars were significant. In the First World War, Australia was not threatened by any adversary. Nevertheless, the country of then only five million citizens rose to the occasion and sent approximately 330,000 volunteers overseas, primarily to be subordinate to and fight for British military leaders under the auspices of a British Empire effort. An incredible total of 60,000 servicemen, almost one out of every five, died during the war. Australia, in its "coming of age," had more men killed in combat in that conflict than did the much larger United States.

World War II witnessed an equally impressive effort, initially associated with the British in North Africa and then later with the Americans in the Pacific. At the start of the war in September 1939, Australia had in all three services about 10,000 regulars and 90,000 reservists. By the end of 1941 the total was 230,000. Royal Australian Air Force (RAAF) strength alone reached 160,000 personnel and 6,000 aircraft, and the RAAF became temporarily the world's fourth largest air force. The ADF peaked at almost two-thirds of a million in uniform by mid-1943 and fell off to 575,000 by war's end in September 1945. (Australia sent 550,000 overseas and lost more than 34,000, including 8,000 in Japanese POW camps.)[8] This total six-year experience affected almost everyone in a nation of about seven million people.

Australian Defense before the Dibb Report

From World War II up to the mid-1970s, Australian defense policy features were generally quite dependent on the United States. Not until the latter time period did any form of defense self-reliance begin to emerge and incorporate itself into a special arrangement of mutual dependency with the United States. In addition, until the middle of the 1970s, no Australian government had made defense the subject of "substantial intellectual analysis."[9] A discussion now follows of the Australian defense features associated first within the ANZUS alliance and then with the alliance aside.

Full-House ANZUS

The term most identified with Australian defense strategy within a full-house ANZUS was that of *forward defense*. The concept for the ADF was not a new one but was applicable prior to heavy commitment to the United States before and after the ANZUS alliance began functioning in the early 1950s. Support for forward defense initially went to the British and gradually shifted over to the Americans. Forward defense began with the dispatch of the Australian Regular Army's 8th Division to Malaysia in mid-1941 and did not end until the final

Australian combat forces withdrew from Vietnam in early 1972. Some argued that a residual forward defense presence (i.e., use of Butterworth Air Base in Malaysia and similar small-scale arrangements) and forms of obligation (i.e., Five Power Defence Arrangement or FPDA) remained in the area. However, most agreed that forward defense in the old sense was unworkable after the last British and US military units withdrew from mainland Southeast Asia in 1975. Apart from World War II there was some discussion that Australian contributions to forward defense and reactions to crises threatening its security interests were not appropriate. A few commentators likened them to "tokenism" and "defense on cheap." [10]

If the above critical or demeaning comments were debatable, indisputable was the traditional Australian insistence about the need to ally with great and powerful friends. Australian ideas about security needs and requirements were slow to change. Factors of geographic location, history, politics, allegiances, and perceived threats all combined to make Australia, at least until recently, willing to accept the role of a junior partner. Although Australians, according to a recent ambassador to the United States, "are not . . . and never will be prepared to adopt a supine and uncritical posture towards their major ally," [11] they have been known to bend and oblige. Australia realized that it had complex and difficult problems in adequately defending its own continent and interests, which covered an area equivalent to the continental United States but with less than 7 percent of the latter's human resources and 4 percent of its wealth.

Despite the difficulties inherent in defending such a vast area, the ADF organization in the past gave low priority to home defense. During the years before 1986, the primary objective was organization for overseas deployment as part of an integrated allied force. The ADF only recently began slowly adjusting to the policy of first preparing to defend the Australian mainland (three million square miles) and the surrounding maritime environment (another three million square miles). At the same time, the ADF wanted to be capable of contributing to ANZUS and its share of the Western security network. [12]

The first instance of ADF units performing forward defense roles under ANZUS was in the Korean War. Although United Nations collective security actions were used to solicit allied military cooperation against the aggressors, the sending of reliable allied Australian forces to fight alongside American ones was an important factor in the United States agreeing to create ANZUS. Australia's immediate readiness to assist the American forces in Korea and the fact that they were the first actually to get into combat made deep impressions.[13]

Australia also participated in forward defense in the Vietnam War. As Australian Ambassador to the United States F. Rawdon Dalrymple pointed out to an American audience in Washington, D.C., "Australia and New Zealand were the only Western allies of the US to join you in the Vietnam campaign." [14] At its height of commitment, the Australian military presence in Southeast Asia reached 8,000, which was a considerable number of servicemen at that time. The costs in casualties and financial expenditure were high. But an even greater cost was the deep division the Vietnam War involvement brought to Australian society. Similar in many ways to dissent and protest against the war in the United States and elsewhere, the Australian connection had another element. For many Australians "the Vietnam debacle effectively killed forward defense." [15]

Australians had not really questioned Sir Robert Menzies' announcement in 1965 of an ADF commitment to the allied cause in Vietnam. Nor had they disputed Prime Minister Harold Holt's famous promise in 1966 to President Lyndon B. Johnson that "you have an admiring friend, a staunch friend, that will be all the way with LBJ." [16] However, after Holt's drowning in late 1967, that particular intuitive understanding between the two governments ended.

By 1968 the questions began with a basic one as of yet never satisfactorily answered: Did the Australian government send troops to Vietnam because of a request from Saigon or because of American pressure to be a reliable ally and support forward defense and ANZUS Treaty obligations?[17] Some Australian observers were critical of this role and considered it one more example of their experiences with the United States in the war with Japan and in the conflicts in Korea and Vietnam. For support, they pointed to several problems in the American record on consultation and cooperation with respective Australian governments. While US officials might have responded differently to the above comments, the views were indicative of past imbalances and disturbances in the bilateral relationship.[18]

Major dependence on US government and private American defense industries for support and equipment has been and will continue to be a basic tenet of Australian defense features. Although proponents of Australian defense self-reliance admitted this was not synonymous with Australian self-sufficiency, there was no contradiction seen in this policy. The ANZUS alliance and its related arrangements were regarded as substantially improving Australia's technical capacities and equipment acquisition processes. The mechanism to provide unin-terrupted supply and other logistics support for the substantial range of weapon systems, high-technology equipment, and other defense material of US origin was a memorandum of understanding (MOU) between the United States and Australia. The latest MOU with a series of appendages on logistics support was dated April 1985. Reviewed each year and preceded by a similar MOU in 1982 and a logistics arrangement in 1965, the MOU set out effective policies and guidelines for logistics support arrangements in peacetime and during periods of emergency. The MOU was the workable cornerstone of equipment support between the two countries. It helped ensure Australia's status as a first-class ally, at least as far as logistics and procurement were concerned.[19]

Table 1 lists ADF aircraft purchased from the United States and illustrates the dominance of American-sourced defense equipment and material in ADF overseas defense expenditure. Primary purchasers of capital equipment have been air, then naval, and lastly ground services of the ADF. The starting point was 1951, when Australia placed with the United States its first large defense order in the post-World War II era. That time also marked both the beginning of the decline in defense equipment acquisition from Great Britain, Australia's traditional supplier, and the formation of the ANZUS defense alliance.

Table 1

Aircraft Purchases (1951 to Present)

Total	US Producer	Name	Type	Remarks
113	North American	Sabre	fighter	redesign (construction under license)
12	Lockheed	P2V-5 Neptune	maritime surveillance	
36	Lockheed	C-130 Hercules	transport	still in service
30	Lockheed	P-3 Orion	maritime surveillance	still in service
20	McDonnell-Douglas	A-4G Skyhawk	fighters	Royal Australian Navy sold remaining 10 to New Zealand
31	Grumman	S-2E Tracker	coastal surveillance	still in service
200 +	Bell, Boeing, Sikorsky, Vertal		helicopters	many still in service
28	General Dynamics	F-111C	strike aircraft	still in service/various configurations
75	McDonnell-Douglas	F/A-18 Hornet	fighter/ air defense	most to be assembled in Australia

Sources: Tom Muir, "The US-ANZUS Partner and Major Defence Supplier," *Pacific Defence Reporter* 12, no. 10 (April 1986): 12; Headquarters US Pacific Air Force, Plans, and Policies Directorate, "Australian Security Assistance Program," (U), 26 February 1987, 1. (Secret) Information extracted is unclassified.

Most analysts agreed that the 1963 decision to purchase the F-111C strike aircraft at the design stage signaled a significant change in Australian policy and a commitment to bring the ADF into much closer association with the United States. The "Americanization" of the RAAF has become all but complete.[20] The bulk of the major equipment purchases falls within the government-to-government foreign military sales (FMS) program. For Australian purposes especially, this arrangement is extensive and important.[21]

Naval equipment purchases, while not as standardized with US systems as the aircraft, are still significant in quality and quantity. The Royal Australian Navy (RAN) formerly used the HMAS *Melbourne*, World War II British *Illustrious*-class aircraft carrier, as its flagship. However, the carrier capability along with its American-sourced, fixed-wing elements of the Fleet Air Arm ended with the *Melbourne*'s "retirement" in 1983.[22] The current process started in the early 1960s, when the RAN purchased three US-built *Adams*-class guided missile destroyers. In the 1970s Australia decided to buy four *Perry*-class guided missiles frigates from the United States and then placed orders for two more such ships, now designated *Adelaide*-class, to be built in Australia. When we combine the number of ships purchased, they make up more than one-half of the RAN's present surface combatant force. The RAAF depends more on US support than the RAN, even though the latter still counts on the United States for quality and quantity.

The Australian Regular Army (ARA), by its nature, does not have big weapons platforms like its sister services. Even so, some of its major equipment, such as armored personnel carriers and two types of howitzer artillery, are of American origin.[23] (See appendix C for equipment details on ADF service branches.)

From the above discussion it is clear that the close relationship with the United States and dependence upon this country for much of its equipment and logistics support make it hard for Australia to be truly self-reliant in defense matters. Unless carefully controlled, the US-sourced equipment, although good for standardization and inter-operability, could channelize defense capabilities. It also could limit Australian defense industry involvement and production capacity. These are the reasons Australian leaders in recent times have emphasized an Australian ability to modify and adapt much of this equipment to meet their own security requirements. For a country like Australia this would still never mean complete self-sufficiency in defense effort. But it could mean, over time, a lessening of dependence on foreign sources—such as the United States—for weapons, supplies, spare parts, ammunition, and so on.[24]

Within a full-house ANZUS, Australia and the ADF continue to play important roles in several other areas. The fact that Australia hosted three joint defense facilities (because of its strategic location as a continent) was probably a noneconomic factor of overwhelming importance to the United States. Although some argued that this arrangement was outside ANZUS, Americans in position of authority generally considered it "within the spirit" of Article II of the ANZUS Treaty (appendix B). The facility hosting and some of the other sensitive military, technical, and scientific agreements between the two countries remained important indicators of close defense cooperation.[25]

More narrowly, Australian security posture necessitates close links with the US intelligence community and access to its relevant raw and finished intelligence and surveillance information. The information flow is a two-way street in which the United States also benefits from Australian-sourced intelligence materials. The Dibb report unequivocally stated that the contribution being made by Australia and the United States to each other's core interests (as in critical intelligence) was a "vital element of symmetry in the security relationship."[26]

There were two other examples during this period of maintaining a commitment to the American alliance through ANZUS. First was the consistent provision of port and air facilities, which supported transiting US nuclear and conventional military forces. The Australian government still has a clear policy to welcome such visits because of alliance responsibility and substantial benefits for its own security. Second was the Radford-Collins agreement of 1951, which also gave justification for combined naval operations.[27]

A final worthwhile element for the ADF in an operative ANZUS was the particular value associated with regular bilateral, trilateral, and participative combined military exercises conducted with full US participation. (For example, appendix D lists the variety of regional exercises ANZUS members had from mid-1982 to mid-1983.) Such extensive and comprehensive exercises as the biennial Kangaroo series in Australia and the Rimpac series off Hawaii have helped to maintain operational skills, evaluate techniques, improve competence, and compare performances. According to Kim Beazley combined exercises with the United States also have familiarized American forces with ADF military capabilities and the operational environment of the region. For instance, each year up to 60,000 US sailors and marines (usually in conjunction with port visits) actively participate with their ANZUS colleagues in exercise operations on and off the Western Australia coast. Improved effectiveness of all forces resulted. Australian officials also know that if the United States does not play in such combined exercises, the opportunity does not readily exist for the ADF, especially the RAAF and RAN, to find suitable replacements for such capable forces.[28]

ANZUS Aside

The focus on Australian defense features is more ambiguous and limited in a setting with ANZUS aside. For years these features have reflected a strategic objective policy that was itself unclear, but was developed in the ANZUS Treaty to provide a type of security insurance guarantee. Yet a major point for many to ponder was the fact that the ANZUS Treaty has never come close to being "tested."[29]

To adjust the reliance and uncertainty, the Australian government's white paper on defense policy in 1976—the year after Saigon fell—created the impression that Australia was trying to be more self-reliant and capable of independent operations. Yet the revised policies did not provide the necessary detailed direction nor ensure the required financial resource allocation to make this policy initiative a reality. Two divergent goals characterized Australian national security objectives at that time. First, the prime intention of the ADF was to support and assist the United States' strategic deterrent and its defense umbrella. Second, ADF needed to have the capabilities to (1) assist in ensuring stability, independence, and strength of its regional neighbors; (2) assist and help protect newly independent South Pacific nations; and (3) continue to play appropriate roles in collective security under

ANZUS, the FPDA (Great Britain, Australia, New Zealand, Malaysia, and Singapore), and other agreements.

Although these were not new concepts, the question remained: Were they achievable? Critics of these defense policies felt then that basic strategic considerations were not the determining factors. What became decisive, however, was the political and bureaucratic contest for scarce funds. A prime example to prove this was the "fortress Australia" mentality shown by the Australian Labor Party (ALP) opposition during the early 1980s debate on funding an aircraft carrier replacement for the HMAS *Melbourne*. Proponents for a new carrier viewed this as a logical and relevant concept of RAN assets to protect vital sea trade routes and promote regional cooperation. The opponents prevailed, and the ADF saw a lessening of its already limited force projection capability.[30]

The ADF had its own military assistance program. The portion dealing with regional cooperation was called the Defence Cooperation Programme (DCP). In recent years, it accounted for about $A 45 million per year, or less than 1 percent of Australia's total defense budget. Of that amount more than 40 percent went to providing nearby Papua New Guinea with military assistance. Whether the DCP was adequate or not depended more on the type of aid than the amount.

Generally, Australian aid in the absence of any single driving purpose (e.g., assistance to Papua New Guinea) was directed at two areas. First, it provided training facilities in Australia for regional members to attend. For example, in 1984 more than 1,000 military personnel from regional countries attended such training courses. Involved within this area were numerous combined exercises and exchanges. Second, the Defence Cooperation Programme allowed ADF serving members to conduct such civil aid missions as mapping, medical assistance, and disaster relief. The bulk of DCP efforts directed toward the South Pacific consisted of such civil aid support.[31]

An extension of Australian military contribution in support of British forces, under the Anglo-Malaysian Defence Agreement of 1957, resulted in the still-in-effect Five Power Defence Arrangement. One aspect of FPDA that stood out was the RAAF's continued use of Butterworth Air Base in Malaysia. It was the largest military establishment used by the RAAF outside Australia. The Integrated Air

Defence System (IADS) was another aspect of the FPDA affecting the two regional members—Malaysia and Singapore. IADS was Australia's contribution of a relatively sophisticated air defense radar network capable of aircraft detection as far out as the airspaces of Thailand and Indonesia. Although complaints recently have surfaced in Australia that the FPDA has not been effective and the costs to Australia are increasing, the arrangement still gives the ADF an opportunity to deploy and exercise outside the immediate area of Australia. It also provides—practically, politically, and symbolically—the remaining permanent Western military "forward base" presence on the Southeast Asian mainland.[32]

The ADF has been involved in other overseas operations. Most prominent were two long-term operations in Southeast Asia: the Malaysian insurgency from the late 1940s to 1960 and the Indonesian "confrontation" period from 1963 to 1965. Both campaigns supported British efforts and occurred prior to ADF participation with American forces in the Vietnam conflict. A more peaceful ADF function performed overseas was the recently ended operation in the Sinai Peninsula as members for almost four years in the Multinational Force of Observers (MFO). This particular arrangement had a helicopter unit composed of RAAF and Royal New Zealand Air Force (RNZAF) personnel and helicopters (110/8 and 35/3, respectively). It was a continuing example of equipment interoperability, common operational doctrine, and quasi-alliance benefits.[33]

The cornerstone of Australian-New Zealand defense cooperation and relations was considered by many to be the ANZAC pact (in recognition of the Australian and New Zealand Army Corps, the combined corps that served with distinction in World War I), the first formal treaty agreement entered into between the two Commonwealth countries. Negotiated during World War II and in effect since 1944, the pact's purpose was twofold: to maintain and strengthen relations between the two countries and to provide a means to exchange views and information on matters of common concern, especially as they pertained to the Southwest and South Pacific areas. From a strictly defense point of view, paragraph 35 of the treaty provided for defense cooperation by means of consultation, common doctrine, equipment and training, staff interchanges, and logistics support coordination. Over the years closer defense and logistics cooperation developed to a point which took into account that, although their defense needs were not quite the same, they were sufficiently parallel to permit a high degree of mutuality. Accordingly, in the spirit of strengthening both countries' military capabilities, a memorandum of understanding was signed in 1983 to develop a common industrial support base.[34]

When all these various factors came into play within and outside ANZUS, it was evident that the proper development of the ADF and a national defense infrastructure for operational deployment in defense of Australia and its several interests was not an easy matter. Australia also had a classic view that saw itself as always assisting larger powers to achieve their goals, being a middle power facilitator, and providing leadership to smaller countries that did not trust larger powers.[35] Whether such a view of Australia's role in international and regional relations was accurate or not, it carried over into discussion on defense policy, alliance relationships, and proper use and structure of the ADF in peacetime and during war. This discussion first started surfacing in the late 1960s to mid-1970s and was associated with several of the main turning points which affected ADF defense emphasis.

Changes in Defense Emphasis

Having considered an active defense alliance with the United States and participation in America's wars to be the fundamental basis for Australian military planning, the Australian government was shocked by several significant events starting in the late 1960s. First was the 1969 Nixon Doctrine. Australian attitudes on security dependence were already changing by 1968 primarily due to disillusionment with the war in Southeast Asia. Enunciation of the Nixon Doctrine and its embellishment by subsequent American administrations, whether appropriately understood or not, sent tremors through the Australian political and military ranks. While not giving Australian defense planners clear-cut alternatives, the doctrine at least added impetus to reorienting defense strategy toward one of increased self-reliance but with continued support for American deterrence and ANZUS.[36]

The Australian Labor Party government of Prime Minister Gough Whitlam in the early 1970s caused Washington to become more aware of Australia as a middle power of growing influence in the region. Whitlam had problems in dealing with the Nixon administration, even though he realized that his country's relations with the United States were all-important. The Whitlam government's cancellation of orders for several major defense capital equipment items, such as destroyers for the RAN, which were to have formed the nucleus of three independent naval task forces, eventually restricted ADF areas of operation.[37] Attitudes and perceptions of powerful leftist groups within the Labor party were also forming, and they brought about, if not a distancing from, at least a readjustment of the close defense reliance on the United States. From roughly this time on, serious attempts to adopt a more self-reliant defense posture began to be made in Australia. Central to this posture was the belief that such future security requirements as low-level military contingencies were in fact national responsibilities and must have main priority in Australian defense policy and planning.

The next shocks came to Australia (and others) with the fall of Saigon, South Vietnam, to Communist forces in 1975 and the concurrent vast reduction of American combat and support forces stationed in Southeast Asia. For Australia, which for years had organized its ADF integration with a larger allied force, the confusion was great. These events combined helped force Australians to contemplate changing the ADF, albeit slowly and hesitantly, through a major restructure.[38]

In a partial reflection of this changed defense orientation, the ADF has taken measures especially in recent times to reduce gradually its already limited involvement overseas. The MFO operation in the Sinai has ended. There have been slow reductions of forces from the permanent assignments at Butterworth Air Base and temporary duty attachments in Singapore. The Dibb report stated that the Five Power Defence Arrangement, including Australian presence at Butterworth, represented the concerns of a previous era. While still useful as a basis for practical cooperation, these overseas arrangements were based on political as well as military considerations.[39] Despite Dibb's opinions,

Australia planned to continue deployments (but at reduced levels) to Butterworth and to military exercises with friends and allies in the area.

Another turning point on defense emphasis started with the election of the Labor government to federal office in 1983. This government, aware of a growing level of public comment on issues of defense and security and armed with thoughts of creating sound and effective defense policy and forces, undertook several important steps. Accepting the fact that a linkage existed between support for an active alliance with the United States and a positive policy on arms control, the ALP new government's initial step was to review ANZUS completely. Second, and almost in parallel, it stepped up diplomatic efforts on arms control issues. Third, Labor party leaders decided to review the ADF with the objective of improving the military's capacity for self-reliance with concentration on the region of direct security concern to Australia.[40]

This latter step was not easily accomplished and, in fact, is still under way. Yet it was a step in the right direction. Momentum for conducting such a thorough review had been building to a decision point in the early 1980s. The trend in defense thinking slowly shifted to the idea that procuring ADF weapon systems and fixing priorities for new equipments, many of which were to have multipurpose roles, needed to focus more appropriately on Australia's own defense needs. Previous determining circumstances for much of Australian weapon system acquisition, use, and planning were governed by the ability to fight wars in distant theaters. That was no longer going to be the deciding factor. What was gradually emerging from the civilian branch of the Defence Department as a guiding theme for ADF emphasis was the balanced requirement for versatility, mobility, and endurance in defense of Australia and its several primary interests.

The means to achieve these objectives found partial attainment in the approach of Paul Dibb's report on defense capabilities done under Defence Minister Kim Beazley's guidance, direction, and authority. Beazley and Prime Minister Bob Hawke (both of whom were Rhodes scholars in their postgraduate days) occupied powerful positions in the right division of the Australian Labor Party and reflected the traditional rightist view of ANZUS and defense: pro-American, fairly conservative, and pragmatic. A native of Western Australia, Beazley was a relatively young (less than 40 years old) and ambitious member of Parliament; some political observers thought he would eventually rise to the top of his country's political structure. He has gained recent prominence by using his academic training in international relations and defense policy to make the minister of defence portfolio appointment highly visible and important in the Labor government. In 1985 Beazley asked Dibb to "examine the content, priorities, and rationale of defence forward planning and to advise which capabilities are appropriate for Australia's present and future defence requirements."[41] The result was the 1986 *Review of Australia's Defence Capabilities*, which the government incidentally stressed was not a statement of official policy but an independent analysis of defense policy issues.[42] Regardless, it marked the final turning point in defense emphasis prior to publication of the 1987 white paper on defense policy.

The Defense Setting after 1986

The Australian defense features associated with ANZUS in a post-1986 setting—after the Dibb report was published—are not much different from those present in the years just prior to the Dibb report. The larger change is in the approach to defense beyond the purview of the ANZUS Treaty.

Revised ANZUS

ANZUS, or more appropriately the revised ANZUS bilateral defense relationship between Australia and the United States, continues to affect most segments of ADF either directly or indirectly. Although Australia has changed significantly the nature of its strategic perspectives and defense priorities, ANZUS remains important to Australia for its role in the global Western alliance network and, perhaps more critically, for its practical benefits for Australian independent defense.[43]

These benefits cover a wide range of important subjects. For Australia, an ANZUS framework means that it keeps intact a firm relationship with a strong and close ally and will work toward fulfilling basic obligations within that relationship. The joint defense facilities are to remain fully functioning, and Australia feels the facilities contribute to the avoidance of global conflict. More germane to ADF are the following issues:

- combined exercises and training;
- high-technology transfer;
- force interoperability;
- material acquisition and support;
- equipment and weapon systems standardization;
- common operational doctrine;
- logistics support arrangements; and
- intelligence and surveillance resources.

Australia also will continue to purchase substantial defense arms and supplies from the United States. Over the next decade, it plans to spend $A 15-20 billion in America. The extensive bilateral agreements and arrangements, coupled with an ongoing series of useful and productive meetings and sessions at several levels, aided much in the effective interaction and improved defense relations. These are all positive aspects of a healthy bilateral relationship.

The United States is willing to continue these cooperative defense endeavors, because it realizes that a capable conventional ADF contributes not only to regional security but also to US security interests and global deterrence. In return, the costs for Australia (excluding the financial aspects) are not high. In light of the problems with New Zealand, this relationship is expected to grow even stronger and more significant in the Pacific region.[44]

ANZUS Aside

ANZUS aside, the ADF is trying to use the strategic lessons taught by the Pacific War portion of World War II and other events to shape its self-reliant capabilities to suit the Australian strategic environment. It expects to go well beyond specific area defense and be involved with aid, cooperation, training, and a host of other defense-related issues. The current defense policy, according to Beazley, is to pursue "a disciplined relationship between strategy and force structure within the constraints of limited financial means. Australia's first priority must be defense self-reliance."[45]

One area of intended expansion is in military assistance programs. These programs reflect a governmental objective to increase activity substantially in the South Pacific region. The government wants to improve its long-standing defense cooperation with Papua New Guinea. The RAAF is increasing the number of long-range maritime patrol (LRMP) aircraft deployments to the South Pacific from five to 10 each year. When planning the RAN fleet program, the navy was endeavoring to have its ships make regular visits to independent countries in the region. Perhaps the most opportunistic area for defense cooperation is upgrading the small island countries' abilities to manage and protect their important exclusive economic zones (EEZ) and land areas, as shown on the accompanying map. Australia has offered to assist several countries in developing the Pacific patrol boat, specifically designed to meet their 200 nautical mile EEZ surveillance needs. A total of 12 boats at an estimated cost of $A 61.7 million are on order. This entire project is far larger than any previous Australian defense cooperation project in the South Pacific region or in Southeast Asia.[46]

Internally Australia plans to adjust to a shift of defense resources from the traditional populated regions of its south and east to the sparsely inhabited north and northwest areas of the continent. It has become clear that the ADF needs to defend many vulnerable installations and resources in these latter more remote areas. Yet the defense (and civil) infrastructure is minimal.[47]

Australia is also trying to improve its defense and logistics support structure. Minister Beazley has made limited headway in setting out some new ground rules for the defense industry. First among the changes is that defense spending, either at home or overseas, must have relevance to the nation's strategic priorities. Second is that defense industry should become commercial in its approach and compete for various projects. Although Beazley's efforts are not revolutionary, they

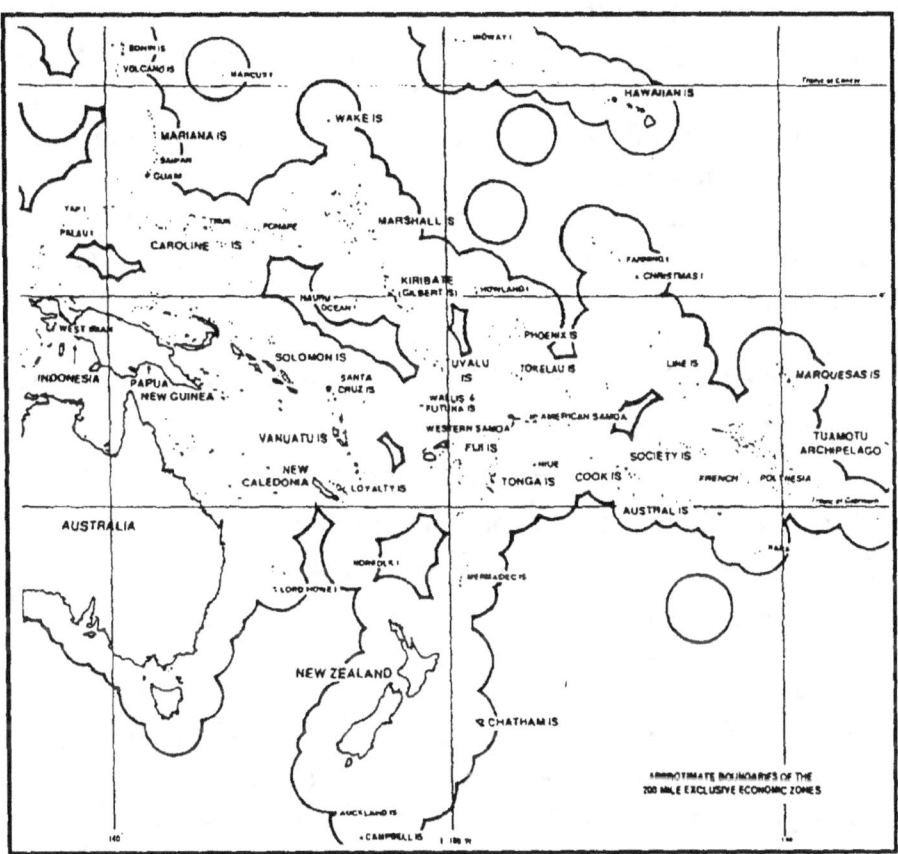

South Pacific Exclusive Economic Zones

Source: Robert Igara, "Economic Cooperation in the South Pacific," in *New Zealand and the Pacific*, ed. Roderick Alley (Boulder, Colo.: Westview Press, 1984), 201.

signaled the likelihood, for the first time in a generation, of a balanced and consistent government policy for the defense industry.[48]

To a lesser degree than before, the ADF will continue to support and to participate in the Five Power Defence Arrangement and the Integrated Air Defence System on the Malay Peninsula. It will increase slightly a defense effort in the Southeast Asia region that focuses on the development of associations and military relationships based on shared concerns. The ADF military assistance program, by means of exercises and training, appears to be more promising than strict adherence to the dated and more formal FPDA.[49]

Finally, ANZUS aside, the Australian-New Zealand bilateral defense relationship will keep on being one of "substance," according to Beazley. Substantive issues include:

- an extensive program of combined exercises;
- high-level consultations;
- cooperative defense procurement;
- logistics and supply cooperation;
- staff and training exchanges; and
- defense science and communications cooperation.

Even though the Australian Labor government recognizes its defense relationship with New Zealand is strong and important, Canberra appears to regard the alliance relationship with the United States as being even more important for security purposes. In a forceful December 1986 speech given in New Zealand, Australian Foreign Minister Bill Hayden said that Australia disagrees completely with New Zealand's nuclear ship ban policy, and he flatly rejected the prospect of being the replacement for the former US role in a defense understanding with New Zealand. Australia is incurring additional and unacceptable expense due to the need to duplicate military exercises and other arrangements with its ally across the Tasman Sea. In this arrangement it remains to be seen over the long term how much the ADF can contribute to and work with the New Zealand Defence Forces.[50]

Review of Australia's Defence Capabilities (1986)

Paul Dibb's independent *Review of Australia's Defence Capabilities: Report to the Minister for Defence* focused on the capability and force structure requirements of the ADF. Dibb admitted that his report contained little new in the way of redirection themes. Instead, for the first time, it brought together the major themes in Australian defense policy that had been under way for the past decade and a half, ever since "forward defense" ended and calls for "defense self-reliance" began. The report created an interesting and informed public debate on defense issues that was both refreshing and necessary for a democracy like Australia.[51] In short, Dibb's study brought about a major shift in Australia's approach to defense.

The basic thrust of the report was to move Australian defense policy in the direction of a more self-reliant posture. Dibb's approach to narrow down the area of judgment relied on two principles. The first one required an understanding of Australia's unique geographical circumstances since the ADF needed to plan on defending the country and national interests on its own. The second principle called for more preciseness in defining the threats Australia faced, with intelligence and warning time figured in. The defense strategy that was needed for these tasks was one of "denial," which in turn would become associated with "layered defence." According to Dibb, this would ensure that an enemy would have substantial difficulty in crossing the sea and air gaps around Australia. The doctrine of "layered defence" and the extended warning time (up to 10 years) for development of a regional assault threat of substance became two of the main sources of contention and misinterpretation about the report.

Another significant aspect concerned definition of the main areas of operation for the ADF. An important and recurring theme was the need to concentrate force-structure priorities in the area of *direct military interest* to Australia. This was where Australia should seek to exert independent military power. The area represented about 10 percent of the earth's surface. It stretched more than 4,000 nautical miles east to west from New Zealand and the Southwest Pacific islands to Australia's Cocos Islands in the Indian Ocean. It was more than 3,000 nautical miles north to south from the archipelagoes of Indonesia and New Guinea to the Southern Ocean bordering Antarctica. The report also recognized a sphere of *primary strategic interest* generally encompassing Southeast Asia and the South Pacific. Dibb felt that this area could affect Australian national security but did not pose any direct military threat. Therefore, ADF structure and priorities should not be oriented toward this greater area. Likewise, being part of ANZUS was important but not a requirement for allied Australia to become involved in US contingency planning for global war.

While there was considerable emphasis on defense strategy and policy, the Dibb report was first and foremost a force-structure document. Minister Beazley directed Dibb to determine what the ADF and its support structure needed for capabilities and requirements as Australia planned for entry into the next century. Dibb held that his report as presented provided a central theme of Australia's being a defensible continent. With some adjusting of ADF structure and priorities, the military would be able to carry out well this national task in the 1990s and beyond. Beazley, as expected, was very supportive of the report since it closely mirrored his thoughts and ambitions. One of the defense minister's major objectives was to convince Australians that they could defend themselves and establish the necessary force structure and organization to make self-reliance a reality. Dibb had assumed a 3 percent annual real growth in defense spending. In that regard his report was of little help to Beazley, who now had the more difficult task of starting the slow but consistent long-term process of logical force development within the strained financial resources of Australia. The *Review* was an important step in laying the groundwork for other developments, such as the white paper on defense policy, to follow.

Dibb brought out several interesting aspects of Australian defense features that were critical if Australia wanted to have some type of effective self-reliance and best use of limited resources. The first dealt with the recently altered ADF senior command structure. With that change much more central power and authority were given to the Chief of the Defence Force (CDF) and the Headquarters Australian Defence Force, similar to the US chairman of the Joint Chiefs of Staff organization. The functional command structure was showing improvement. The individual service chiefs were shifting from former roles of being sole commanders of their components to being more a part of the three operational commands centered on the Headquarters Australian Defence Force. The CDF was using direct responsibility to delegate aspects to those functional commanders handling maritime defense, air defense, and land defense. The RAN, RAAF, and ARA remained as separate services, but they ideally were working more closely together than in the recent past. Although individual services were unwilling to lose their separate planning functions, each service realized that most functions would eventually rest with a central and pivotal coordinating body. Joint planning and operations were expected to show improvement over the current arrangements.[52]

Other parts of the Dibb report dealt with the very important and often-neglected areas of defense industry and logistics support—the "tail of the dragon." Concerning defense industry, Dibb criticized the relative inefficiency of most government defense factories and encouraged future defense industry growth in the private sector. He established three capability guidelines for the Australian defense industry. They included the need to:

- repair, maintain, and modify most defense force equipments, especially those associated with low-level contingencies (e.g., the type Australia would face);

- produce high-usage spare and ammunition items, if not excessive in cost; and

- design and produce in those areas of unique national requirements or where domestic capacities were clearly competitive on an international basis.[53]

Even though government policy, the requirement for an improved defense industry policy as spelled out in Dibb's comments needed to receive increased attention. This seemed especially worthwhile because current ADF defense expenditure within Australian industry represented only one-half of 1 percent of the gross national product (GNP). Most knowledgeable commentators agreed that Australian defense requirements would still need considerable support and supply from overseas, mainly from the United States. Absolute self-sufficiency was neither realistic, justified, nor sought under present and future circumstances.

Dibb's coverage of logistics support requirements was good. Excluding manpower costs, logistics support activities in Australia accounted for more than one-quarter of defense outlays each year. The extensive inventory totaled more than 1.6 million line items, was worth several billion Australian dollars, and was managed by more than 30,000 military and civilian personnel. Additionally, ADF logistics support involved more than 15 million transactions annually, which was an important part of defense requirements that had to be flexible, sustainable, and economical. One of Dibb's recommendations was to shift more defense resources to the northern and northwestern portions of Australia. But implementing that recommendation would exacerbate the logistics problem since the infrastructure in that part of the continent was poor and the majority of support and supply bases were located thousands of miles away.[54]

Many prominent and influential Australians praised the Dibb report because it provided for the first time a positive and identifiable task for the ADF. One of its more enthusiastic supporters was Air Chief Marshal Sir Neville McNamara, who had recently retired as CDF. To Sir Neville, the report was a "serious and well-reasoned attempt to bring together all major considerations relating to development of a self-sufficient ADF although there is nothing glaringly new in the report." He went on to say,

> Drawing together of Australia's interests, strategic circumstances and defence priorities should greatly assist in promoting greater understanding of need for appropriate measure of defence capability. Definition of area of direct military interest and sphere of primary strategic interest, together with proposals for meaningful strategy, layered defence concept and recommendations for relevant capabilities should provide a most useful working basis for development of the Government White Paper and more positive guidelines for benefit of defence planners.[55]

Although the air chief marshal was generous in praising the report, his predecessor as CDF, Adm Sir Anthony Synnot, was not. Admitting the report was well researched and credible, Sir Anthony found fault with the strategy of denial. He saw it as being too defensive and reacting only to what an enemy might do first. His alternative was a strategy of deterrence, which rested on the existence of a believable threat of unacceptable counteraction. It implied offensive capabilities that had to be seen at all times to be able to hit a potential enemy where it was going to hurt most severely. Sir Anthony still found truth in the adage, "Offence is the best form of defence." [56] Air Vice Marshal Tony Mason, a Royal Air Force representative to a mid-1986 Australian conference on air power, said the same in a slightly different way.

> It is a truism of war that a good defence can avert defeat, but seldom if ever impose a political solution upon an enemy or, more simply, secure a victory.[57]

Others were even more critical of the report. Peter Henderson, the immediate past permanent head of the Australian Department of Foreign Affairs, perceived isolationist trends. He feared that in trying to attain the overdue and totally commendable degree of independence and self-reliance in defense, Australia might find itself disengaged from the close and necessary ties now enjoyed with the Western alliance in general and the United States in particular. Henderson wanted more attention paid to military power projection capability into the sphere of prime strategic interest and more effective "integration with allied (that is US) forces." [58]

Another critic was Michael O'Connor, executive director of the Australia Defence Association, who found Dibb guilty of "situating the appreciation," and making "facts" fit a set of preconceptions. Feeling that there was a complete rejection of the idea that Australia should make contributions to the defense of allies and friends, O'Connor thought strongly that Dibb proposed a classical fortress strategy. Despite Kim Beazley's protests to the contrary, in O'Connor's mind this approach was wrong since "no such fortress has ever yet survived a siege." [59]

A criticism of strategic naval aspects came from A. W. Grazebrook, an Australian who has written often on naval matters affecting his country. It was clear to Grazebrook that the Dibb report, perhaps using the Strategic Basis as guidance, substantially underestimated the importance of overseas trade to Australia's economy and thus the need for a capable navy to defend that trade. Since Australia directly traded some 30 percent of its gross domestic product (GDP) with other nations, disruption of maritime trade would become significant in the long term.[60]

As a final example of Australians being upset with the Dibb report, Peter Samuel, a Washington-based journalist, provided some pessimistic comments. Writing in *Strategic Review*, he envisioned Australia's meaningful and active participation in Western defense planning and operations ending if recommendations in the report were taken. Consequently, there would be a drastic redefinition downward of Australia's defense alliance obligations. To counter this, Samuel urged the United States to "reject Dibb [before] it becomes part of Australia's conventional wisdom about defense." [61]

What were the official and unofficial American reactions to the Dibb report? Perhaps the most concern about the report's implications came from the US Navy. It appeared to be no accident that Adm James Lyons, then commander of the large US Pacific Fleet, was the first American official to criticize the report publicly.[62]

Former government officials were also willing to speak out. Former US Assistant Secretary of State for East Asia and Pacific Affairs and later US ambassador to Indonesia John Holdridge said that it was a mistaken strategy for the Australians to zero in on defending northern Australia from low-level to midlevel forays by northern neighbors. "Who is going to attack from island-nations in the north?" Holdridge also worried about increasing Soviet pressures and threats to Western influence generally in the Pacific. He questioned Australia's intentions to contribute to an "all for one, one for all" concept of Western security.[63]

Richard Armitage, US assistant secretary of defense for international security affairs, issued a more moderate official public reaction. In a statement prepared for broadcast to Australia, he said the Dibb report "appears to be a serious attempt 'to fit' defense policy, forces, and strategy into a 'rational mix.'" As he diplomatically put it, the report was an attempt to harmonize the very difficult problems of working out defense policy, force strategy, and the final objectives.[64]

The most significant American response was seen at the extra session between Defence Minister Beazley and US Secretary of Defense Caspar

Weinberger during the August 1986 bilateral American-Australian meeting in San Francisco. Subsequent to the meeting, Beazley and other Australian officials stressed that the Dibb report essentially was only a force-structure document and not official Australian policy. It would be an important influence, but not the only influence, on the upcoming government white paper on defense policy. Australia would take into consideration a number of factors, to include Dibb's recommendations and US concerns as the government formulated its positions in the white paper.[65]

Government White Paper

Australia's long-awaited defense white paper, *The Defence of Australia 1987*, was released in March. As expected, it picked up the main thrust of the 1986 Dibb report, yet still satisfied the Americans, conservative commentators, and the Australian military, who had found objectionable certain aspects of the Dibb report. Despite little emphasis on protecting sea lines of communication, the policy paper did tone down suggestions arising from Dibb that a "fortress Australia" was opting out of regional responsibilities and out of the Western strategic community. To show that some of the earlier American concerns were now at rest, Adm Ronald J. Hays, United States commander in chief, Pacific Command, wrote in an advance release that

> Australia is developing a comprehensive strategy for structuring, equipping, and training its defense forces. Australian strategic studies, force modernization, and reorganization stressing joint operations will improve Australia's military capability and therefore promote regional stability.[66]

What was in the white paper to make Admiral Hays think this way? The tone of it was set early in the preface. Defence Minister Beazley started out strongly by stating that the Australian people expected Australia to provide for its own security. Defense self-reliance in depth still had to be achieved within a framework of alliances and regional associations. It was a multiple-way arrangement in which the support of alliance and associations made such self-reliance attainable. In turn, a self-reliant Australia gave them support since it would be able to better meet Australian responsibilities within its own strategic region.

According to Beazley, the concept of self-reliance being used to set the course for a decade of development achieved the four basic objectives of Australia's national and international defense policy. The objectives were to (1) develop and maintain a capacity for independent defense; (2) promote regional strategic security and stability; (3) strengthen the ability to meet mutual obligations shared with its primary allies, the United States and New Zealand; and (4) improve Australia's ability as an active member of the West to contribute to strategic stability at the global level. These were not new fundamental objectives. The 1976 defense white paper identified self-reliance and its objectives as a primary requirement. Yet that white paper failed to give appropriate substantive direction to the concept. Beazley's *Defence of Australia 1987* intended to correct those deficiencies by setting clear goals and by providing the comprehensive overall approach to Australian security that would result in responsible defense planning.

The white paper then defined Australia's present and future defense interests as follows:

- defense of Australian territory and people from military attack threat;
- protection of Australian interests in surrounding maritime areas, offshore islands, and close-by ocean areas and vital choke points;
- avoidance of global war;
- maintenance of a strong defense relationship with the United States;
- furtherance of a favorable strategic situation in Southeast Asia and Southwest Pacific;
- promotion of a sense of strategic community between Australia and other countries in areas of direct military interests; and
- maintenance of Antarctic Treaty provisions.

These interests fell naturally in line with the basic defense policy objectives.

As outlined in the white paper, the primary tasks of the ADF were to carry out the first two interests above: defense of Australia and protection of its interests in the area of direct military concern to the nation. Accordingly, Australia planned to make a number of changes. Chief among them were proposed efforts to strengthen northern defenses, create a two-ocean navy, get a credible mine countermeasures capability, and develop an integrated air defense capability. In addition, Australia wanted to continue to cooperate closely with allies. The new-look ADF would have improvements in range, endurance, mobility, and independent logistics support.

To budget for all these requirements, Australia was going to devote more than 33 percent of the defense budget over the long term to the largest capital investment in the country's peacetime history. This intended allocation amounted to more than $A 25 billion (approximately $US 17 billion at 1986 exchange rates) spread over 15 years. What remained uncertain was how Australia could accomplish all these objectives within a budget allocation of 2.6 to 3 percent of GDP, which corresponded to slightly less than 10 percent of governmental outlays.[67] As Karl Jackson, the US deputy assistant secretary of defense for East Asia and Pacific Affairs, pointed out in a congressional hearing, the present government of Australia was indeed showing a strong commitment to defense and alliance with the United States. Since one of its keystones of security was a strong economy, Australia's future defense posture would require steady and consistent budget allocations, based on a strong economic structure, to be effective. Although his program is ongoing, only time will tell if Beazley's ambitious ADF improvement and development program will stay on schedule and within resource constraints.[68]

The overall thrusts of the white paper were to meet the governmental requirements for basic competence and preparation in matters of national defense and to provide for Australia's own security and for its defense activities and influence. The country's policymakers believed that the planned development of the ADF, as discussed in the 1987 white paper, was in step with Australia's security needs. Planned ADF development, *if properly carried out* (e.g., funded), would accomplish first and foremost the priority task of defending the nation. The important secondary tasks of ensuring that an enemy would find it difficult to use force against Australia and allowing for Australia to make realistic contributions to regional security and alliance activities also would be achieved.[69] As Thomas-Durell Young, an astute American observer of ANZ defense matters, pointed out, "Overall, the 1987 Australian defense review must be assessed favorably from the viewpoint of Western interests. . . . in positive terms."[70]

Present and Future Service Capabilities

For discussing the present and future ADF service capabilities, a logical starting point is the new concept of a central command and control organization embodied in the Chief of the Defence Force, the Vice Chief of the Defence Force (VCDF), and Headquarters Australian Defence Force. More authority and control formerly resided in the individual air force, navy, and army services. Since its 1984 redesignation, the top military officer no longer is Chief of the Defence Force Staff (CDFS) but heads a newly created Headquarters Australian Defence Force. The CDF now commands the ADF, with direct staff support being provided by Headquarters ADF, which in turn and, in conjunction with the service offices, undertakes operational military planning for the CDF. Under these arrangements single service chiefs of staff retain their command responsibilities and also provide combat-ready force elements to joint force commanders.

The ADF now emphasizes the areas of joint operations and planning. In 1986 the government created the appointive office of VCDF. That same year the ADF appointed air, maritime, and land force commanders and started to develop supporting operational headquarters and doctrine. The joint force commanders report directly to the CDF and have responsibility for the conduct of designated joint ADF exercises and operations. As an example of the new arrangements, the ADF is beginning to set up a separate joint-force command, headquartered in Darwin, Northern Territory, to support increased ADF activity and basing in remote northern and northwestern Australia.[71]

Institutions already in place and others in various stages of development have facilitated increased ADF joint planning, operations, support, instruction, and training. To improve in the joint arena, the ADF has for instance the joint theater command structure (of which Darwin is a proposed test bed), the Joint Intelligence Organization, and the Joint Warfare Establishment.[72] In the instruction and training areas, the ADF maintains the Joint Services Staff College for senior-level officers (of which there is usually an American field grade officer on each six-month course), and the recently opened Australian Defence Force Academy. The ADF Academy, on the grounds of the Royal Military College Duntroon in Canberra, trains officer candidates for each of the military services.

Air Force

The easiest way to look at the service components is to start with the air force, because it is the military branch most satisfied with the current and planned ADF development. With 22,800 airmen on active duty, the RAAF is capable, improving, and arguably the most effective air force in the region. Under the white paper statement of policy, the RAAF would mainly be concerned with activities involving air and maritime warfare.

By far the most significant recent event affecting the RAAF was the introduction of the F/A-18 Hornet multirole tactical fighter aircraft into the inventory. Labeled by Gordon Scholes, Beazley's predecessor as defence minister, as the "largest single defence project ever managed in Australia," the F/A-18 program has dominated ADF's equipment planning for several years.[73] The reason is that Australia assembled in-country, at a rate of 18 aircraft per year, a total of 73 of the 75 advanced high-technology fighters, designed and produced by the US-based McDonnell-Douglas Corporation. The arrangement called for Australia, under its Australian industry participation (AIP) program, to form an integral part of the Hornet aircraft modification and assembly. The program has gone well. The state-of-the-art, high-technology Hornets replaced the French-designed and Australian-built Mirage III-0 all-weather interceptors, first introduced into the RAAF more than 20 years ago. The Hornets are now operational, with three squadrons (two at RAAF Base Williamstown in New South Wales with several aircraft, aircrews, and support on temporary duty at Butterworth Air Base in Malaysia, and one at the new RAAF Base Tindal in the Northern Territory).

Two other RAAF aircraft programs are also important. F-111 aircraft are the only legitimate long-range aircraft the RAAF has for strike and interdiction, since the F/A-18 is used primarily for air defense. Australia's 23 F-111s are being refurbished, at minimum cost, to reduce operating costs and maintain the aircraft in service. The government feels that more F/A-18s, configured as dual seaters for attack, can be purchased later to replace F-111s lost through attrition. Critics argue that F-111s, and not F/A-18s, need to undergo expensive upgrading because they, along with the RAN's submarine force, are the only real ADF elements with primary strike and interdiction missions and capabilities. A second major aircraft program is the continued capabilities improvement, by acquiring modern electronic support measures, of the 20 US-produced P-3C Orion long-range maritime patrol aircraft.

Despite the healthy picture of capital equipment gains, RAAF leaders still feel they have some real shortcomings affecting the air power portion of the ADF. To perform its role as a first-line defense, the RAAF requires several additional enhancements. According to retired Chief of Air Staff David Evans, the most serious problems are the lack of "force multipliers" like inflight aerial refueling and airborne early warning and control aircraft, inadequate contingency stocks of munitions, and the continuing severe shortage of trained pilots and aircrews. To this list is added the need for new tactical airfields in the north. To correct some of the problems, the Australian government plans to modify its four Boeing 707 aircraft for inflight refueling and is building a chain of northern air bases, as highlighted by the new RAAF Tindal Air Base—the designated home for one of the new F/A-18 squadrons. Yet progress is slow and expensive. One of the most serious issues as yet uncorrected is the permanent departure of skilled manpower resources from the RAAF.[74]

Navy

The Royal Australian Navy is also undergoing changes. Partly due to the 1983 decommissioning of Australia's only aircraft carrier, HMAS *Melbourne*, and the demise of the fixed-wing element of fleet air arm, the RAN was down to an active strength of 15,700 personnel. In terms of maritime security the white paper proposed several RAN upgrades. It would divide the navy into two fleets, one deployed in the Pacific and the other in the Indian Ocean. To support the eastern-based fleet, the RAN possibly planned to relocate certain fleet facilities from Sydney to Jervis Bay, farther south on the coast. For the Indian Ocean-focused forces homeported in the west, the RAN would expand its naval base at Stirling, south of Perth, Western Australia.

The RAN intends to improve its limited mine countermeasure (MCM) force, as long neglected in Australia as in Western navies elsewhere. In Australia's case, it has the option to procure the new Australian-designed *Bay*-class catamaran inshore minehunter, assuming that its first of class trials proves operationally successful. The expressed need for more MCM capabilities is a step in the right direction.

In the area of surface combatants, the present government wants to expand the existing major surface combatant force of 12 destroyers—three guided missile destroyers (DDG), four guided missile frigates (FFG), and five destroyer escorts (DE)—to an operational force of 16 to 17 major surface combatants. Planning calls for a naval force able to respond to three broad levels of capability. The DDG and FFG high-capability surface combatants comprise the top level. A new class of vessel, the light patrol frigate (also known as the new surface combatant), would provide the second level of capability. That new class of eight frigates would represent the largest peacetime ship-building program ever in Australia and would replace the DE class currently in RAN. Patrol boats suitable for coastal operations would maintain the third level. Assuming that all the planned developments for the surface combatants occur, the allied fears sparked by the Dibb report of lack of commitment for ADF maritime elements should be eased.

To be a meaningful and effective deterrent, a fully implemented maritime strategy for Australia needs mobility and afloat support; versatility; interoperability with other ADF components, allies, and regional friends; and offensive and defensive capabilities. An expanded RAN surface force able to deploy on a regular and consistent basis to the outer maritime areas is essential for this strategy.

The RAN also plans to replace its submarine force of six *Oberon*-class, diesel-powered submarines with a newer class of diesel submarines in the 1990s. The submarines were selected to have Swedish-designed Kochums A Type 471 external hulls and would be built and fitted out in Australia. They would homeport on both coasts. The new submarine construction project will be costly (more than $A 3.3 billion) and complicated. Yet there are many Australians who see the submarine project as a logical extension of an Australian capability to master increasingly complex programs and as the type of project to be encouraged in Australian industry. In addition, it would help ensure greater ADF independence and self-reliance.[75] As the RAN project director, RAdm Oscar Hughes, analyzed it, the submarine program is taking Australian industry "three or four rungs up the ladder." [76] Hughes said that

> Australia has never before attempted a project of this magnitude and scope. To make it all work, we are looking for four to five fold increase in the numbers of companies achieving acceptable levels of quality assurance and the Navy has already embarked upon a national quality control familiarization program for industry.[77]

Unlike the F/A-18 program, which consisted of modifications and assembly of already designed parts, the submarine program requires that 60 to 70 percent of the content, including the design work, be carried out in Australia.

The RAN is not without problems. One of these concerns diminished antisubmarine warfare (ASW) capabilities. With the retirement of the RAN's sole aircraft carrier, the navy lost the ability to send to sea its Sea King helicopters, which supplied medium-range ASW capabilities. The RAAF now has the responsibility to provide fixed-wing air support to the fleet at sea. Included within this arrangement is the need for the RAAF P-3C Orions to conduct ASW operations. Yet the P-3C aircrew force is grossly undermanned. The RAAF's 20 Orions are expected not only to support the fleet but to fly maritime surveillance along Australia's 11,000 nautical mile coastline and out into its maritime areas of strategic interest. The ASW problem needs attention and correction soon.

While there remains a blue ocean capability for fleet operations despite the *Melbourne's* departure, it is different from what it used to be. The Australian government appears to be indicating a partial shift of strategic interests from Southeast Asia to the South Pacific. Evidence is seen in the RAN port visits in 1987 in which 27 port calls were planned for the general South and Southwest Pacific region and only five to specific Southeast Asian ports. Concurrently there was an almost complete pullback of RAN ships providing support to US Navy task forces in the northwest Indian Ocean and Persian Gulf areas. The RAN said such deployments were using 11 percent of its annual fuel commitment. Those deployments to the far Indian Ocean are now over. The policy instead is to show a greater presence in the near eastern Indian Ocean. When the US Navy is in that area, the RAN will try to conduct combined exercises with it at sea. Yet even this reduced-presence plan is doubtful. For example, the RAN announced a plan to send a six-ship task force to the South China Sea in 1986, first for an FPDA exercise and then to a follow-on exercise with the US Navy. One month later, the Australians canceled all plans due to lack of funds. Some observers saw this as a sign of things to come.

Finally, like the RAAF, the RAN has a continuing problem of retaining skilled personnel after training. There is already a chronic shortage of personnel to effectively man the *Oberon*-class submarine squadron with its six boats. Combined with the overall RAN cutback in authorized personnel, the sea-going service has a serious manning problem. One wonders, given the present circumstances, how the RAN expects to man a fleet that will expand significantly in the 1990s.[78]

Army

According to the white paper, the Australian Regular Army will put more emphasis on highly mobile forces capable of rapid deployment.

This shift appears to bode well for soldiers serving in the infantry or helicopter support and somewhat less so for those in armor or artillery. Despite a reduction of almost 700 men, the army has the largest manpower component, with an active force of more than 32,000 and a reserve complement of around 25,000 of various levels of skill and proficiency. The white paper contained several changes of emphasis for the ground force. The government's policy is that, in response to the wide range of credible contingencies, the army structure must have highly mobile forces capable of rapid deployment anywhere within Australia and its territories. This force structure requires no major organizational changes from the current army one based on the 1st Division (mostly regular), two reserve divisions (2d and 3d), and Training and Logistics Commands.

The mainstay for army rapid deployment in low-intensity operations will continue to be the 3,000-man-strong Operational Deployment Force (ODF), based in Townsville, northern Queensland. The ODF formed itself from the army's 3d Brigade, 1st (Infantry) Division. This unit is really the only organization in the land force ready to go into real combat with just a few weeks' warning. Organized with a rough 5:4 ratio of combat soldiers to support (including light artillery, communications, and so on), the ODF receives priority in army allocations.

An area that is getting increased attention is the important one of support. The consolidation of all ADF helicopters into the army partially addressed the issue of direct combat support. This consolidation included both battlefield and utility helicopters, some of which over time were to be transferred with personnel from the RAAF. To increase lift capability, the army intends to acquire at least 36, and possibly more, American-built Blackhawk helicopters. They would supplement the 30 UH-1H helicopters (also American-built) already in ADF service.

Part of the army's problem is to ensure it has an adequate base capable for quick, sufficient expansion when a military threat becomes apparent. The army wants to improve the state of its reserve forces to fill this need. To increase reserve participation, some of the armored and mechanized formations are being shifted to the reserves. Critics of this move stress the importance of such formations in any major land operations in defense of Australia, and thus the need for state-of-the-art capability to be maintained in a core (e.g., regular) ground force. This issue requires further resolution.

Finally, it is necessary to stress another problem area for the Australian ground forces which is possibly the most serious of all. The problem is the same as that bothering the RAAF and RAN, loss of skilled manpower. Some refer to it as a "crisis of confidence." Others say the problem is discontent caused by low pay and poor living and family conditions. Figures from the first half of 1986 illustrate the high number of qualified officers resigning from the ADF. In the first quarter of 1986 the resignation rate jumped by 46 percent from the year prior and in the second quarter 47 percent. More than 1,000 officers left the active service in an 18-month period. At a time when the ADF is undergoing major restructuring for the future, a high loss rate of skilled professionals—due to low morale, poor pay, and so on—becomes even more serious. Not just in Australia's but in any country's effective defense force, the foundation rests on having good, qualified, and dedicated career personnel.[79]

Logistics Support and Defense Industry

An adequate defense logistics support structure and a capable defense industry are unglamorous but important factors that Australia must accept and deal with if defense self-reliance is to be achieved. The Labor government realized this and used the 1986 Dibb report and the 1987 white paper to highlight such special challenging areas inherent in defense of Australia.

Some commentators on the present logistics support system have been free with their criticisms. Maj Gen J. D. Stevenson, head of the Australian army's logistics operations in the early 1980s, doubts that adequate logistics support for even a modest force with a limited operational commitment can be provided without bringing the rest of the ADF to a standstill. This "worst case" even allows for time to develop an operational capability. Stevenson believes that the ADF faces the following logistics problems in meeting modest requirements:

- remoteness of possible operation areas from the main support areas in southeast Australia;
- limited civil-logistics infrastructure in the operational areas;
- inadequate transportation infrastructure in or along the route to the possible operational areas;
- inadequate major repair facilities and limited availability of spare parts and component replacements; and
- inadequate operational logistics organization.[80]

Despite this unpromising outlook, all is not lost. Government officials and others are at least trying to address some of these difficult and long-standing challenges. One example is the recently published series of articles in a book titled, *A Vulnerable Country? Civil Resources in the Defence of Australia.* The editors were Dr Desmond Ball and Col J. O. Langtry of the Australian National University's Strategic and Defence Studies Center in Canberra, Australian Capitol Territory. Prime Minister Hawke provided a foreword. The book rightly notes that the sheer size of Australia poses enormous defense planning and logistics problems that are compounded by limited and concentrated resources. A way to help alleviate these problems is to have a national railroad system. Especially important for defense of northern Australia to a medium-level military threat is completion of the 1,000-mile Alice Springs-Darwin rail link. It would directly benefit national development and defense, including the new F/A-18 facility at Tindal Air Base. Nevertheless, the rail network limitation is just one of many serious logistics problems. Australia must keep on trying to solve these involved and expensive (estimated $A 1 billion for the rail link alone) logistics support challenges.[81]

The continued vitality of the defense relationship with the United States is the most important element of the external realities affecting Australian defense logistics support and industry. The United States is the major source, and in many instances the only source, for much of the ADF's advanced defense equipment and technology. The memorandum of understanding on logistics support renegotiated in 1985 contributed substantially to Australian defense support capabilities. It formed a fundamental part of the strong alliance relationship that promoted favorable terms and improvements for both countries. An example of benefits derived from such an arrangement was the successful Nulka project, which was a major collaborative equipment effort between the two countries. Nulka was a joint project established between Australian defense science and technology organizations and the US Navy to design and produce an antiship missile defense system.

The defense industry itself has room for improvement. On the government's side the science and technology capability of the Department of Defence is concentrated in the Defence Science and Technology Organization (DSTO). With a total staff of 4,300, DSTO has more than 16 principal locations scattered throughout Australia, and it contributes to the development and implementation of Australian defense policy by the direct application of science and technology. DSTO provides assistance to the ADF, Department of Defence, other defense agencies, and even private industry.

DSTO's current and future programs include many activities specifically designed to increase Australia's self-reliance on defense. One of the most interesting and expensive DSTO projects is the indigenous development of an over-the-horizon (OTH) radar system known as Jindalee, an aboriginal word meaning bare bones. Originally begun as a proposal from the Australian Weapons Research Establishment in 1969 and approved in 1974 with the first long-term allocation of funds, Jindalee now consists of one large radar facility near Alice Springs providing broad area air surveillance. Eventually, a Jindalee network, if feasible and affordable, of up to three radars will be a basic element of a national air defense and control system. Current planning is for one or two to be sited in north or northeast Australia and one in the west or southwest. Whatever its final outcome, Jindalee promises to enhance Australia's air defense alert and early warning capabilities.[82]

Private defense industry plays an important role in meeting the government requirement for defense self-reliance. Paul Dibb was correct in dismissing complete self-reliance since Australian requirements for complex systems and weapons (e.g., tactical fighter aircraft and air-to-air, air-to-ground, and ground-to-air missiles) dictate a need for overseas suppliers. To make this workable some primary overseas sources are building branch offices in Australia. For instance, the American Raytheon Corporation established an air-to-air missile facility near Sydney that began operations in 1987. Yet Australian defense industry could still get a significant share of the internal market. In 1985-86 the ADF spent more than $A 2.8 billion on activities directly relevant to defense industry. Of that amount, almost one-half, or $A 1.3 billion, was spent in Australia. The potential is there for increasing that figure over time.

One means to improve internal involvement is the Australian industry participation program. The AIP is an integral part of the F/A-18 modification and assembly project for the RAAF. The AIP program structure provides Australian industry the capability to work with military resources to enable self-reliance in engineering, maintenance, and spares provision. The AIP and an effective defense offsets program are important for a viable defense industry, especially when working with US corporations involved in long-term projects like the F/A-18 Hornet acquisition program.[83]

While there is promise—some already demonstrated and some still being talked about—in the important areas of logistics support and defense industry, much more needs to be done. One area demanding attention and action is to build and retain a skilled manpower resource in-country. Government and private policies, backed by consistent investments and flexibility, are also necessities for long-term improvement. The present government apparently understands these basics and is attempting to correct some deficiencies and achieve a more balanced approach.

Federal Budget Requirements

The provision of adequate resources for the defense of Australia is essential. However, defense spending cannot be determined in isolation from Australia's other national priorities and economic circumstances. The 1986-87 federal budget cut real growth in defense expenditure to 1 percent, with funds increasing by $A 743 million to a total of $A 7.415 billion (about $US 4.9 billion). This represented 9.9 percent of government outlays and 2.9 percent of GDP. It was in keeping with the government's plan to spend approximately 3 percent GDP per year on defense.

Defense outlays have gone up and down in past years. The outlay peaked at well over 4 percent of GDP during Australia's heavy involvement in the Vietnam War. Since then the outlay has been from 2.6 to 2.9 percent. As related to government expenditures, the annual outlay rose from a low of about 8.4 percent in the mid-1970s, following the end of Australia's "forward defense" participation in Southeast Asia, to about 9.5 percent in the early 1980s and to 9.9 percent now. If applied steadily and evenly, these figures appear correct for ADF defense features in peacetime. The fact that Australia is spending on defense about 319 US dollars per capita is just a fair measure of the political process that was behind the defense expenditure proportion of the federal budget.

In the 1986 financial year, the defense expenditure breakout was as follows:

- capital equipment, 28 percent;
- capital facilities, 5 percent;
- personnel, 40 percent; and
- operating costs, 27 percent.

As far as major capital equipment expenditure goes, the high costs for the F/A-18 aircraft and FFG-class frigates will wind down on program completions. Yet expenditures should remain considerable since other major capital equipment projects will then begin, such as new submarines, mine countermeasure vessels, light patrol frigates, more helicopters, and OTH radars. One expenditure must remain the highest—that for personnel. Despite such outlays the problems associated with low pay and benefits persist. They in turn create the single biggest problem for the ADF: the continued loss of skilled manpower from the three military services, the reserve, and the civilian defense work force. Any lessening of this allocation could produce very serious results for the Australian Department of Defence.[84]

Australian and New Zealand Defense Relationship

Australia and New Zealand share a defense relationship that has a degree of importance to the security of both countries. Concerns include a common history, proximity, and shared strategic interests. New Zealand has an important role to play in the South Pacific. In some cases it has been more substantial than or at least equal to Australia's. Australian and New Zealand defense forces need to develop and maintain their ability to operate together. Where practical, affordable, and on its own terms, Australia plans to continue defense cooperation with New Zealand and improve operational capability.

In the unresolved dispute between New Zealand and the United States over visits by ships, understanding the present problems is not enough. Australia officially is not a party to the disputes and is on record as saying that New Zealand's political policy on nuclear bans is wrong. Australia will continue working with New Zealand on defense and other issues of mutuality in a revised ANZUS period. Yet there is only so much the ADF can do for and with the New Zealand Defence Forces. A return to the ANZUS security situation that existed before the dispute is desirable but doubtful. Accordingly, the defense relationship between the antipodean neighbors will neither suffer greatly nor improve significantly in the present political and economic environment.

Growing Australian and US Defense Relationship

To the surprise of almost no one, the 1987 white paper came out very positively for a strong bilateral defense relationship with the United States. Australia accepted its roles as part of the Western community of nations, as an active member in the ANZUS defense alliance, and as a provider for its own defense self-reliance. This mature, modern approach coming from such a close ally was one which the United States readily welcomed. Australia purposely tried in its white paper to accommodate some of the American concerns evident with the earlier Dibb report. Both countries acknowledged the considerable benefits enjoyed by each in a special security relationship.

The ANZUS Treaty and its related agreements, such as the joint defense facilities, all remain in effect. Australia is more than willing to work with the United States on a variety of defense matters as a demonstration of its commitment to deterrence and self-reliance with close cooperation. Australia's alliance with the United States is and should remain a genuinely equal partnership. Their solid bilateral defense relationship is expected to continue and most likely grow even more.[85]

Summary

The Australian Defence Force has earned a reputation for being capable and dependable, especially during wartime conditions. Its peacetime performances have fluctuated. These shifts have been evident both inside and outside the prevailing ANZUS security structure. Partly due to an expressed need to be more self-reliant in defense matters and to a revised policy of more regional security orientation—versus the former one of forward defense— Australia has in recent years attempted to change its defense features.

Several major events have shaped these adjustments. One of the most significant was the notable *Review of Australia's Defence Capabilities* (the Dibb report of 1986), which basically examined future ADF structure. Following this was the comprehensive government white paper, *The Defence of Australia* 1987, which laid out defense policy by incorporating not only key points of the *Review* but also American concerns and desires for collective security. The end result was an Australian position which sought and was likely to attain an even stronger and closer bilateral defense relationship with its close ally, the United States, regardless of what form the future ANZUS alliance had. Unknown, however, were factors affecting Australian ability to provide for its considerable program of defense improvements and enhancements. Among the most serious problem areas were service operational capabilities, federal funding, logistics support, relations with New Zealand, and probably most important, departure of skilled military personnel.

The overall Australian effort has potential and is generally moving in the right direction as far as Australian—and American—political and military leaders are concerned. However, much more disturbing are the changes that the former third partner in ANZUS—New Zealand—is going through. Alliance problems concerning defense and security issues are serious and have gone beyond the divisive nuclear ship ban issue. The next chapter looks at New Zealand, the main Western security influence in the South Pacific region, in the context of its many changing defense features.

Notes

1. Gerald Varni, "ICA Exclusive Interview—The Honorable Kim Beazley, Australia's Minister of Defence," *International Combat Arms* 5, no. 2 (March 1987), 82.

2. Ibid.; J. L. Millhouse, "Australia's Security beyond the Year 2000—The Importance of Asian-Pacific Economic Cooperation," *Journal of the Royal United Services Institute*, November 1984, 33.

3. P. Lewis Young, "International Defense Profile: Australian Defense Forces," *International Combat Arms* 5, no. 2 (March 1987): 68.

4. Ross Babbage, *Rethinking Australia's Defence* (St. Lucia, Australia: University of Queensland Press, 1980), 217.

5. *The Bulletin* survey was discussed by T. M. Hawkins, "Public Perceptions of Defence in Australia," *Journal of the Royal United Services Institute*, June 1985, 13-15.

6. T. B. Millar, "Australia and the United States," in *Australia's External Relations in the 1980s: The Interaction of Economic, Political, and Strategic Factors*, ed. Paul Dibb (Canberra, Australia: Croom Helm, 1983), 155; idem, "The Defence of Australia," *Daedalus* 114, no. 1 (Winter 1985): 260; Fedor A. Mediansky, "Threat Perception in the Southwest Pacific Region: An Australian Perspective" (paper presented at the National Defense University Conference on Pacific Basin Security: Impact of Political and Social Change toward Year 2000, Honolulu, Hawaii, 27 February 1987), 15; Andrew Mack, "Crisis in the Other Alliance: ANZUS in the 1980s," *World Policy Journal* 3, no. 3 (Summer 1986): 449.

7. Robert A. Brand, "Australia, New Zealand, and ANZUS," *Atlantic Community Quarterly* 22, no. 4 (Winter 1984-1985): 350.

8. Millar, "Defence of Australia," 260-61; Dalrymple, 583; N. F. Ashworth, "Time, Gentlemen, Please," *Pacific Defence Reporter* 12, no. 12 (June 1986): 15; Terry Gwynn-Jones, "The Royal Australian Air Force," *Air Force Magazine* 68, no. 8 (August 1985): 67, 70.

9. Harry G. Gelber, "Australian Strategic Perspectives" (paper presented at the National Defense University Symposium on Trans-Pacific Security Issues, Honolulu, Hawaii, 29 May 1980, 12.

10. Millar, "Defence of Australia," 265, 267, 270; Mack, 452; F. Rawdon Dalrymple, "On Being a Superpower's Ally: The Case of Australia," *Australian Foreign Affairs Record* 57, no. 7 (July 1987): 585; P. Lewis Young, 68.

11. Dalrymple, 585.

12. Millar, "Defence of Australia," 265, 267, 270; Mack, 452; Dalrymple, 585.

13. J. G. Starke, *The ANZUS Treaty Alliance* (Melbourne, Australia: Melbourne University Press, 1965), 33; Joseph M. Siracusa and Glen St. John Barclay, "Australia, the United States, and the Cold War, 1945-51: From V-J Day to ANZUS," *Diplomatic History* 5, no. 1 (1981): 48, 50.

14. Dalrymple, 584.

15. Ibid.; Millar, "Defence of Australia," 271; Andrew Mack, "Australia's Defense Revolution," *Journal of Defense & Diplomacy* 4, no. 9 (September 1986): 5.

16. Dalrymple, 584; Millar, "Defence of Australia," 271; Mack, "Australia's Defense Revolution," 5.

17. Dennis L. Cuddy, "The American Role in Australian Involvement in the Vietnam War," *Australian Journal of Politics and History* 28, no. 3 (1982): 340, 344-45.

18. Fedor A. Mediansky, "The United States and Australia: Some Comments on a Reflection," *Australian Outlook* 31, no. 1 (April 1977): 122.

19. Alan Burnett, "The Discontinuous Triangle," n. p., 1978, 31; idem, "ANZUS Triangle: Defence and Security," n. p., 1978, 35. Tom Muir, "The US-ANZUS Partner and Major Defence Supplier," *Pacific Defence Reporter* 12, no. 10 (April 1986): 13.

20. Muir, 12; Burnett, "ANZUS Triangle," 32.

21. "Australian Security Assistance Program" (U) (Headquarters US Pacific Air Forces: Plans and Policies Directorate, background paper, 26 February 1987), 1. (Secret) Information extracted is unclassified.

22. Thomas-Durell Young, "Down Under White Papers," US Naval Institute *Proceedings* 114, no. 3 (April 1987): 140.

23. Burnett, "ANZUS Triangle," 33.

24. Paul Dibb, "Issues in Australian Defence," *Australian Outlook* 36, no. 3 (December 1983): 163.

25. Burnett, "ANZUS Triangle," 24; Andrew Clark, "Hawke Gets the Message that American Farmers Come First," *The Bulletin* 108, no. 5516 (29 April 1986): 26.

26. Fedor A. Mediansky, "Australia's Security Outlook and the American Alliance," *Asian Defence Journal*, October 1986, 56-57.

27. Michael O'Connor, "Fundamental Weaknesses in Australia's Defence Policy," *Pacific Defence Reporter* 12, nos. 6/7 (December 1985-January 1986): 213; Varni, 80.

28. Varni, 80; Robert A. Brand, "Defence Down Under: An American View," *Pacific Defence Reporter* 11, no. 12 (June 1985): 14; B. White, "The Defence Link

across the Tasman," *Journal of the Royal United Services Institute*, November 1984, 63.

29. White, 62.

30. Thomas-Durell Young, 137; John Davidson, "Security and Lines of Communication in the Pacific and Indian Oceans" (paper presented at the National Defense University Symposium on Pacific Security, Washington, D.C., 20 May 1981), 144; Michael O'Connor, "Australia's Retreat into Isolationism," *Asian Defence Journal*, December 1982, 76.

31. O'Connor, 77; idem, "Australia's Regional Defence Cooperation," *Asian Defence Journal*, August 1985, 93, 96; Ray Sunderland, "What Is Australia's Defence Strategy?" *Journal of the Royal United Services Institute*, November 1984, 15; "Statement by the Minister for Defence: The Hon. Kim C. Beazley, MP, on Defence Initiatives in the South Pacific," 20 February 1987, 2; S. Thana, "Australia's Defence Perspectives: A Review on the Way," *Asian Defence Journal*, April 1984, 61.

32. Thana, 56, 58.

33. Burnett, "The ANZUS Triangle," 8-9; Brand, "Defense Down Under," 13.

34. White, 62; Thana, 61.

35. Dibb, 103; David Fulghum, "Foreign Officers Study Dynamics of Alliances," *Air Force Times*, 8 December 1986, 49.

36. Clive Williams, "Better to Deter Than to Defend," *Pacific Defence Reporter* 12, no. 12 (June 1986): 18; Henry S. Albinski, *The Australian-American Security Relationship: A Regional and International Perspective* (St. Lucia, Australia: University of Queensland Press, 1981), 7.

37. Joseph M. Siracusa, "Australian-American Relations, 1980: A Historical Perspective," *Orbis* 24, no. 2 (Summer 1980): 276; David Barnett, "Substance or Symbolism: The Dilemma for Radical Hawke," *The Bulletin* 108, no. 5514 (15 April 1986): 30.

38. P. Lewis Young, 68-69.

39. Paul Dibb, *Review of Australia's Defence Capabilities: Report to the Minister for Defence* (Canberra, Australia: Australia Government Publishing Service, 1986), 48. Hereafter referred to as *Review*.

40. Burnett, "The Discontinuous Triangle," 28.

41. Dibb, *Review*, v.

42. Dibb, "Issues in Australian Defence," 163-64; Mack, "Australia's Defense Revolution," 5; idem, "Crisis in the Other Alliance," 459; Varni, 82; Ian Hamilton, "No 1—Most Testing Period Ahead," *Pacific Defence Reporter* 13, nos. 6/7 (December 1986-January 1987): 200.

43. Ross Babbage, "The Future of the Australian-New Zealand Defence Relationship" (paper presented at a seminar on New Zealand Defence Policy, Institute of Policy Studies, Victoria University, Wellington, New Zealand, 9 December 1986), 4; Dibb, *Review*, 46.

44. US Department of State, telegram, subject: Revised Transcript of Joint San Francisco Press Conference, 230606Z August 1986, 3, 7; Dibb, *Review*, 46.

45. Varni, 80; "Defence Initiatives in the South Pacific," 2.

46. "Defence Initiatives in the South Pacific," 2, 5-7.

47. Andrew Robertson, "Wars Not Won by Defence Alone," *Pacific Defence Reporter* 13, no. 3 (September 1986): 14; P. Lewis Young, 79.

48. "Defence and Industry: A New Deal," *The Bulletin* 108, no. 5526 (8 July 1986): 72.

49. Dibb, *Review*, 48.

50. Varni, 80; American Embassy, Canberra, telegram, subject: Foreign Minister Hayden's Arrival Statement in Wellington, 100320Z December 1986, 1; United States Information Service, American Embassy, Wellington, telegram, subject: Media Reaction, 110351Z December 1986, 1.

51. Babbage, 6; Mack, "Australia's Defense Revolution," 5.

52. Dibb, *Review*, v, 3-5, 176; John Edwards, "Secret Report: We'll Go It Alone with Fast, Hit-hard Forces," *The Bulletin* 108, no. 5513 (8 April 1986): 25-28; John Stackhouse, "Defence 86—Going It Alone," *The Bulletin* 108, no. 5526 (8 July 1986): 59, 61-62, 65; idem, "Defence Brass Prepare for Infighting," *The Bulletin* 108, no. 5513 (8 April 1986): 26-27; idem, "The Dibb Repellent," *The Bulletin* 108, no. 5523 (17 June 1986): 26; *The Defence of Australia 1987* (Canberra: Australian Government Publishing Service, 1987), 60.

53. Dibb, *Review*, 101, 107-9, 112; Ross Babbage, "Implications of Dibb Report for Defence Industry," *Pacific Defence Reporter* 13, no. 3 (September 1986): 35; J. D. Stevenson, "No 2—Logistic Support Demands More Attention," *Pacific Defence Reporter* 13, no. 4 (October 1986): 35, 48.

54. Ibid.

55. Sir Neville McNamara, "No 1—A Serious Guide to Future Defence," *Pacific Defence Reporter* 13, no. 4 (October 1986): 32-34.

56. Sir Anthony Synnot, "No 1—Basic Strategy Is Wrong," *Pacific Defence Reporter* 13, no. 2 (August 1986): 17-18.

57. Robertson, 15.

58. Peter Henderson, "Isolationist Trends in Dibb Report," *Pacific Defence Reporter* 13, no. 3 (September 1986): 8-9.

59. Ibid.; Michael O'Connor, "Australia's Defence Policy: Making the Facts Fit the Conclusion," *Asian Defence Journal*, June 1986, 10, 14; idem, "Dibb's Siege Mentality: The Counter View," *The Bulletin* 108, no. 5526 (8 July 1986): 68, 71; idem, "Fundamental Weaknesses in Australia's Defence Policy," 214.

60. A. W. Grazebrook, "No 2—Errors of Major Significance," *Pacific Defence Reporter* 13, no. 2 (August 1986): 19.

61. Peter Samuel, "The Dibb Report and Australia's Defense Vagaries," *Strategic Review* 14, no. 4 (Fall 1986): 47, 53.

62. Fedor A. Mediansky, "Washington Startled by Roaring Mouse Down Under," *The Bulletin* 108, no. 5544 (11 November 1986): 119.

63. Howard Handleman, "Whither Australia? U.S. Has Major Reservations about Dibb Report," *Pacific Defence Reporter* 13, no. 2 (August 1986): 45.

64. Ibid.

65. Peter Samuel, "Weinberger Criticizes Report Recommending Australian Defense Policy Changes," *Defense News*, 10 November 1986, 28.

66. "Defence White Paper," *Pacific Defence Reporter* 13, no. 10 (April 1987): 19-20.

67. *The Defence of Australia 1987*, vii-x, 2, 19-22; "Defence White Paper," 21; Hamilton, 200.

68. Statement of Karl D. Jackson, deputy assistant secretary of defense for East Asia and Pacific Affairs, in House Committee on Foreign Affairs, *United States Policy toward New Zealand and Australia and the Current State of ANZUS: Hearings before the Subcommittee on Asian and Pacific Affairs*, 99th Cong., 2d sess., 25 September 1986, 5-6.

69. *The Defence of Australia 1987*, 112; "Defence White Paper," 20.

70. Thomas-Durell Young, 141.

71. *The Defence of Australia 1987*, 59-61; "Defence White Paper," 22.

72. While on an exchange officer tour with the RAAF, the author attended in 1982 a two-week field grade officer course at the Australian Joint Warfare Establishment, RAAF Base Williamstown, New South Wales. He was the first US Air Force officer enrolled in that type of course, an orientation program for joint and combined conventional war fighting.

73. T. D. Bridge, "Australian Defence under Hawke," *Army Quarterly and Defence Journal*, April 1984, 150.

74. Ibid.; Gwynn-Jones, 67-68; Special Correspondent, "No 3: RAAF Happiest of Defence Forces," *Pacific Defence Reporter* 10, nos. 6/7 (December 1983-January 1984): 257; F. W. Barnes, "F/A-18 a Major Plus, But Little Progress in Real Defence," *Pacific Defence Reporter* 12, nos. 6/7 (December 1985-January 1986): 224-27; *The Defence of Australia 1987*, 51-52, 64; "Defence White Paper," 22; Robertson, 13; "The Growing Watchful Eye on Our North," *The Bulletin* 108, no. 5553 (January 1987): 56.

75. *The Defence of Australia 1987*, 62-63; "Defence White Paper," 21.

76. Tom Muir, "Submarines and Self-Reliance," *The Bulletin* 108, no. 5526 (8 July 1986): 76.

77. Ibid.

78. A. W. Grazebrook, "No 2: The Navy No Longer a Credible Force," *Pacific Defence Reporter* 10, nos. 6/7 (December 1983-January 1984): 251; idem, "The RAN: The Decline Continues," *Pacific Defence Reporter* 12, nos. 6/7 (December 1985-January 1986): 219, 222; Dora Alves, "A Meaningful Maritime Strategy for Australia," *Pacific Defence Reporter* 13, no. 3 (September 1986): 11; John Stackhouse, "New Subs Survive Attack," *The Bulletin* 109, no. 5560 (10 March 1987): 57-58; Henry Keys, "Why Australia Build Is Worth the Extra Cost: The New Submarine Project," *Pacific Defence Reporter* 13, no. 3 (September 1986): 38; Tim Griggs, "Australia: New Security Perspectives and Policies," *International Defense Review* 19, no. 5 (May 1986): 580; Thomas-Durell Young, 137-40; idem, "'Self-Reliance' and Force Development in the RAN," *US Naval Institute Proceedings* 112, no. 3 (March 1986): 161; Confidential Australian government

source, interview with author, March 1987; discussion with one US military official, March 1987.

79. *The Defence of Australia 1987*, 53, 57, 90-98; idem, "Defence White Paper," 22, 59; P. Lewis Young, 69; Thomas-Durell Young, "Australia's Defense Priorities and Programs," *International Defense Review* 19, no. 5 (May 1986): 583; John Edwards, "How We Can Defend Ourselves," *The Bulletin* 108, no. 5517 (6 May 1986): 54; Brand, "Australia, New Zealand, and ANZUS," 350; Stackhouse, "Defence 86—Going It Alone," 65; J. D. Stevenson, "Army—Skilled, Dedicated, But Denied Adequate Means," *Pacific Defence Reporter* 12, nos. 6/7 (December 1985-January 1986): 216-18; idem, "A High-Quality Army, But No Means to Do the Job," *Pacific Defence Reporter* 10, nos. 6/7 (December 1983-January 1984): 248-49; David Barnett, "Officers March from a Dilapidated Force," *The Bulletin* 108, no. 5539 (7 October 1986): 26; confidential Australian government source, interview with author, January 1987. (Most criticism of the shift came from the Australian Regular Army career soldiers associated with the armored and mechanized branches.)

80. J. D. Stevenson, "The Logistic Problem: It Must Be Faced," *Pacific Defence Reporter* 10, no. 8 (February 1983): 22-23; Hamilton, 200.

81. Ibid.

82. *The Defence of Australia 1987*, 35-36, 65, 69-72, 85; P. Lewis Young, "Project Jindalee: Australia's OTH Backscatter Radar," *Asian Defence Journal*, February 1985, 59-62; Chris Sherwell, "Jindalee Takes Australian Defence by Storm," *Financial Times*, 10 February 1987, 4.

83. *The Defence of Australia 1987*, 89; P. Lewis Young, "International Defense Profile," 73; "Defence and Industry: A New Deal," 72; Special Correspondent, "No 3: RAAF Happiest of Defence Forces," 257; Tom Muir, "Vicissitudes and Achievements in Defence Offsets Program," *Pacific Defence Reporter* 12, no. 10 (April 1986): 4, 10; Brand, "Australia, New Zealand, and ANZUS," 352.

84. Hamilton, 200; *The Defence of Australia 1987*, 99-100, 103-5; Babbage, "The Future of Australian-New Zealand Defence Relationship," 15; Peter Young, "Marching in the Right Direction," *The Australian*, 7 January 1987, 1.

85. *The Defence of Australia 1987*, 3-6; "Defence White Paper," 20-21.

Chapter 4

New Zealand Defense Features

For New Zealand then, the aim in the future will be to have flexible, highly professional [defence] forces capable of operating in our own [South Pacific] region . . . we do not propose to militarize the Pacific.

—Frank O'Flynn, New Zealand Labour Minister of Defence, 1985

Our [New Zealand] armed forces are . . . small . . . but they can hold their heads up in any company in the world . . . effective . . . professional . . . we mean to keep them that way; we must.

—D. Ewan Jamieson, Air Marshal, Royal New Zealand Air Force
ex-chief defence force staff, 1986

Military isolation imposed on New Zealand by United States in reaction to Wellington's anti-nuclear stance has hurt defence forces and would continue to affect them.

—New Zealand defence ministry written statement to
parliamentary committee, 1986

For years, many Americans were not very informed about New Zealand. Those who did know something about the South Pacific nation often had only a vague idea of what the country was like. They knew New Zealanders were friendly, spoke English, and were allies in the Australia, New Zealand, and the United States (ANZUS) defense alliance, which provided collective security in the Southwest Pacific region. Some even knew that the New Zealand military man was usually referred to in a nonderogatory manner by his Western alliance partners as a "Kiwi," just as he considered his Australian counterpart an "Aussie" and his American one a "Yank." Although the New Zealand defense contributions to ANZUS and to Western security might have been small, they were proportionate. New Zealand gave its fair share and in return received benefits from the arrangement.

But in the past 15 years, New Zealand has been going through a transition in most of the fundamental aspects of its national security and well-being. It has created what Dr Dalton West, a Canadian-born New Zealander now living in Washington, D.C., has called the "general security dilemma." [1] Simply stated, the dilemma meant that the greater success New Zealand had in deterring potential aggressors, the greater difficulty it had in defining the need to do so. In the pursuit of national security, the paradox became evident. The more New Zealand chased it, the more elusive it appeared. As Dr West viewed it, the fewer obligations New Zealand was willing to accept in its pursuit of national security today, the more commitments the country assumed in its name. [2]

The dilemma caused New Zealand to undergo many significant changes in its defense features and conditions. This chapter looks at the changes in two settings. First is the one that takes into account New Zealand defense contributions inside and outside an ANZUS alliance prior to the David Lange Labour government election in 1984. Second is the period after that election, from 1984 to the present, which considers New Zealand's defense conditions outside ANZUS only. Australia's middle role comes into focus here. Next comes a review of the extensive two-year cycle of defense debate—beginning with the interim defense review in 1985 and ending with the government's white paper on defense policy in 1987—followed by the current and projected New Zealand Defence Forces' (NZDF) capabilities and shortfalls. Finally, American perspectives on recent New Zealand defense features and conditions are given.

The Historic Role of
New Zealand Defence Forces

New Zealand is a small subregional power and leader in the South Pacific community. It is insulated and isolated by oceans, and it was one of the world's first social welfare states. While the present population of 3.3 million is predominantly white, the racial composition is quickly changing. Indigenous Maoris of Polynesian origin comprise almost 12 percent of the population. The growing influx of thousands of Pacific islanders—Samoans, Tongans, Fijians, and others—is becoming so significant that by the year 2000 every third or fourth New Zealander will likely have a Polynesian ancestor.

Agriculture is the backbone of New Zealand's economy, and international trade is an important part of it. With upwards of 70 million sheep, New Zealand is the world's largest exporter of wool. Despite the direct or support nature of the agriculture-based economy, New Zealand is very urbanized. More than 80 percent of its people live in the few major metropolitan areas, the largest by far being the greater Auckland area at the tip of the North Island.[3] (See accompanying map of New Zealand.)

NZDF, with its several elements, totals more than 25,000 military and civilian personnel. Of this aggregate, 12,600 comprise the active duty force. The military reserves include 2,900 regulars and 6,400 territorials. The civilian portion consists of almost 3,200 government employees connected with the Department of Defence. The defense forces' present size, composition, and capabilities make it a medium-technology conventional force in the South Pacific region.[4] (See appendix E.)

To really comprehend the traditions and history of the NZDF prior to the country's 1951 entry into ANZUS and even afterward, one must understand New Zealand's strong ties with Great Britain. Most of the white New Zealanders were of British origin. Only a generation ago the country still served as "England's farm." More so than neighboring Australia, many in New Zealand fondly called England "home," whether they had ever been there or not. Consequently, for years, NZDF committed itself to a supportive approach to collective security that was distinctively British in nature. New Zealanders demonstrated their unswerving support in wartime by not thinking about their own defense and strategic situation but only of service to the mother country.[5]

Wartime experiences in the twentieth century illustrate this allegiance. In the First World War tiny New Zealand called up 124,000 military members for overseas and home service. Almost 92,000 were volunteers. Of the total, 100,000 went overseas to Europe. In the Second

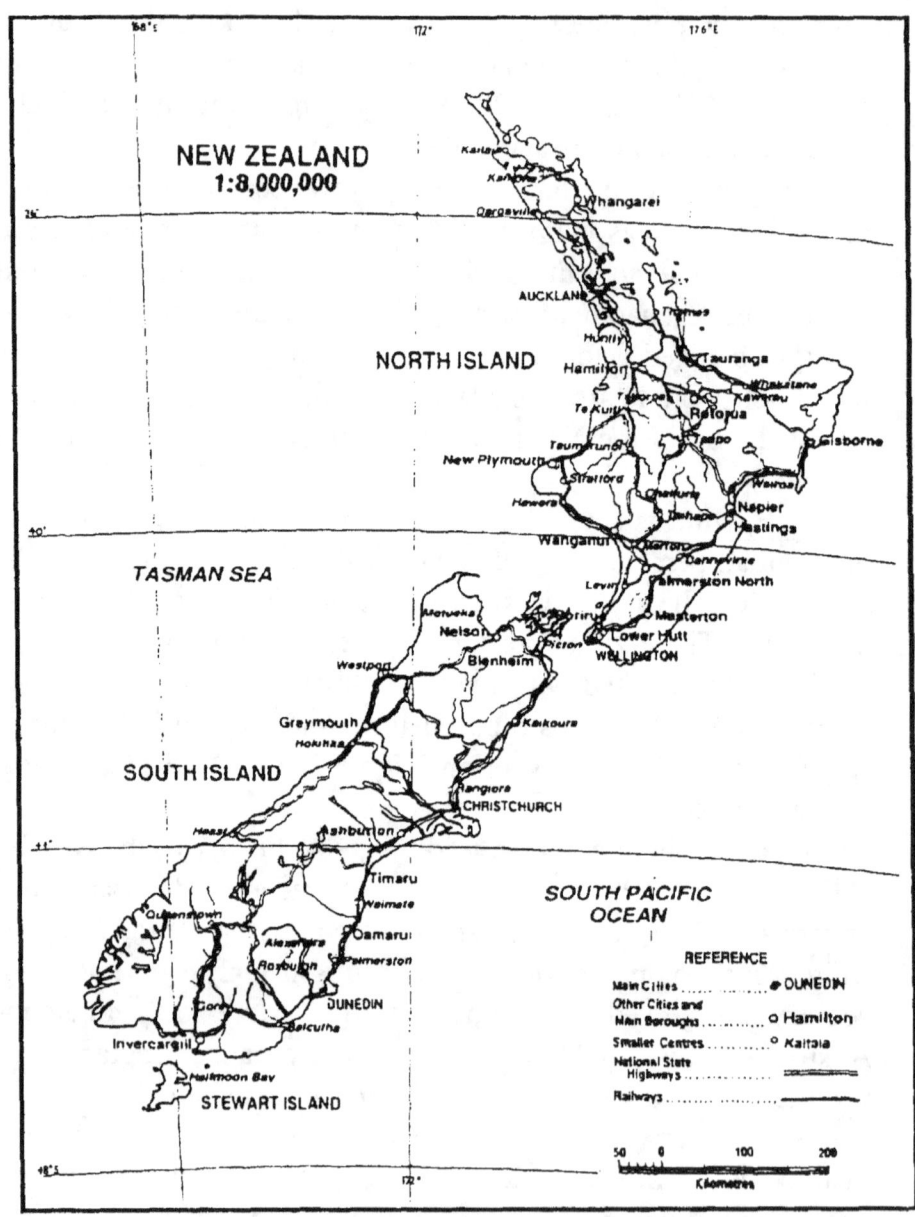

New Zealand

Source: S. H. Franklin, "The Social Structure and Population," in *New Zealand and the Pacific*, ed. Roderick Alley (Boulder, Colo.: Westview Press, 1984), 4.

World War almost 194,000 men and 10,000 women served in the military between 1939 and 1945. The male equivalent was 67 percent of the population of men aged between 18 and 45 years. Over 140,000 served overseas. In the 1950-53 Korean War, a total of 3,200 Army personnel, all volunteers, served in the Commonwealth Division in Korea. Another 1,300 sailors were continuously afloat in Korean waters. Even during the Vietnam conflict from 1964 to 1972, more than 3,800 NZDF personnel had active service in Vietnam. Although this military involvement was ostensibly in response to American requests, it still was representative of the past proven performances of the NZDF in overseas conflicts, mostly in support of British interests.[6]

Following the gradual lessening of British influence in the Pacific after World War II and the withdrawal in the late 1960s of British forces stationed east of Suez, New Zealand (like Australia) switched its supporting defense role. No longer was the role directed toward Great Britain. Defense relations with the United States took on greater importance. For years the defense efforts were sufficient for New Zealanders to know that they were one of the few genuinely liberal democracies totally committed to the Western alliance. As Air Marshal Sir D. Ewan Jamieson, former chief of the NZDF, pointed out, "We have no history of neutralism."[7] Others might have disagreed with the air marshal's comments being applied to present and future national security policies of the Lange Labour government. Few could argue, however, that New Zealand defense efforts in the past were definitely supportive of British defense needs and objectives.

Pre-Lange Labour Government Setting (1952-84)

Like the Australian Defence Force 1,500 nautical miles away, much of the NZDF efforts in the early and middle years of the ANZUS alliance was geared to satisfying the objectives of forward defense. New Zealand's defense strategy, like Australia's, proceeded from the basic assumption that its military operations would be conducted as part of an allied effort under the leadership of a major power. In the 1950s and 1960s, forward defense was a concept that made sense. Accordingly the

NZDF provided a supporting role within ANZUS that closely followed the dictates of preparing to fight away from its own territory.[8]

This approach led to a commitment for NZDF either to be deployed overseas or to be ready to go if the situation required. During US congressional hearings on the American-New Zealand dispute, American government officials emphasized how the two allies had fought side by side in four major wars. New Zealand leaders commented that the overseas involvements were generally due not to the United States but to British Empire-Commonwealth commitments. The fact remained that there was American-New Zealand defense cooperation during times of conflict before and during the ANZUS years.[9]

A number of specific areas were indicative of the considerable involvement New Zealand had in a full-house ANZUS. From its beginnings in the early 1950s, the ANZUS Treaty grew to represent a defense relationship much broader than that provided by the treaty itself. On a functional basis for New Zealand, ANZUS included intelligence-sharing, combined military exercises, training courses, seminars, staging facilities for military aircraft, and port access for ships. These aspects were similar to those of Australia but at a proportionately reduced level. The end result was an easy familiarity that characterized the military-to-military relationship among partners. As Karl Jackson, the US deputy assistant secretary of defense for East Asia and Pacific Affairs, noted, it was a "remarkably integrated trilateral relationship." [10] ANZUS for years remained the cornerstone of New Zealand foreign policy with a security guarantee that was inherent not with the "promise of the ANZUS Treaty but with the premise of the alliance." [11]

The close intelligence relationship between the United States and New Zealand (and also Australia) was one of the most solid fundamentals of a full-house ANZUS. In fact, the small but professional New Zealand intelligence community was and still is for the most part one of the country's strongest supporters of the United States.[12] The intelligence flow went in both directions. The United States was willing to send large amounts of first-rate intelligence information and materials to its ally in the South Pacific. The amounts were significant. NZDF senior military leaders responded in 1986 to a parliamentary select committee that the 80 percent drop in US-provided intelligence, since the 1984 Lange Labour election, severely hampered the military's ability to give up-to-date military information. In return for the heavy American flow, New Zealand provided very useful intelligence and assessments on South Pacific regional issues not available otherwise to the United States. Both sides benefited from the involved and accepted arrangement.[13]

Another important aspect of strong bilateral and trilateral defense cooperation in the ANZUS framework was interoperability, or the ability of the NZDF to operate within and alongside allied formations. Interoperability enabled the modest NZDF to maintain higher standards and operational efficiency than otherwise possible. The NZDF was able to gain access to and be a part of military doctrine formulation, communications, standardization of procedures, logistics, training, defense cooperation, exercises, and the like. These all constituted practical manifestations growing out of the ANZUS alliance relationship which was at times more important than the treaty itself. The New Zealand military was able to develop and maintain its professional competence by working closely with larger partners. The defence force leaders were aware and appreciative of this special situation.[14]

Perhaps the greatest peacetime area in which the NZDF contributed positively was in their small but important support of the 1951 Radford-Collins agreement. As Thomas-Durell Young has consistently pointed out, Radford-Collins is still relevant in maintaining effective maritime control and protecting shipping interests in the region. The agreement, probably more than any other, had a fundamental impact on the NZDF structure, since it required New Zealand to maintain a certain level of forces in peacetime to carry out its maritime obligations and responsibilities.[15]

Since New Zealand's regional defense environment was primarily maritime, the country devoted resources during this period to obtain an interoperable capability to maintain effective maritime control primarily in New Zealand waters and in the South Pacific. The results were seen in the naval and air branches of the NZDF. The Royal New Zealand Navy (RNZN) acquired from Great Britain *Leander*-class frigates to satisfy this objective, and the Royal New Zealand Air Force

(RNZAF) flew American-built A-4 Skyhawks and P-3 Orions to provide maritime strike and surveillance capabilities, respectively.[16] These approaches were in line with later remarks by an NZDF senior military leader on the important role small countries as well as large ones had in keeping a security balance. There was an obvious security role for New Zealand in the South Pacific region.

New Zealand had some workable arrangements for defense logistics support and supply. It had both a memorandum of understanding (MOU) on logistics support with the US Department of Defense (renewed in 1982 but not in 1987) and mutual development of logistics and defense industrial infrastructures with Australia. These were important allied arrangements which would enable New Zealand to obtain needed equipment and supplies, especially during times of sustained operations.[17]

Of particular value was the MOU with the United States. It was an example of a defense cooperation program established in the context of broader alliance activities. In the MOU the US Department of Defense wanted to ensure uninterrupted supply to New Zealand of numerous American weapon systems and other logistics support. In return, New Zealand agreed to provide assistance such as maintenance and refit of transiting American military ships, aircraft, and related equipment. This type of MOU was one of only a few offered by the United States to close allies. Its ending in 1987 meant that New Zealand would no longer receive the special preference reserved for allies in buying weapon systems and parts. The NZDF would still be able to buy the same directly from American manufacturers and through the foreign military sales system but without preference. Although this arrangement was workable, it made such acquisition more difficult for the NZDF. Especially affected was the air force, which was the most "Americanized" among the services in terms of equipment and systems. To emphasize the extent of this dependence, approximately 60 percent of all RNZAF purchases in 1981 were from US sources. The MOU's demise affected the more British-equipped navy less and the army— equipped and supplied mostly by Australian and local sources—least of all.[18]

Full-House ANZUS

New Zealand's contribution to a full-house ANZUS took several forms. From an official perspective, its most obvious symbolic contribution to the alliance was in allowing allied warships continued access to New Zealand's port facilities. On a larger strategic deterrence dimension, Adm Ronald J. Hays, US commander in chief, Pacific Command, stated that New Zealand for years played a role by actively contributing in the policy formulation of the Western security alliance and the ANZUS alliance. Some people observed that the number of US Navy vessels which visited New Zealand (at a rate of seven to eight per year in the early 1980s) was small. Others, especially in New Zealand, argued that the smallest partner's contributions to ANZUS were more than just hosting ships.[19]

New Zealand's perspective on the benefits derived from partnership in ANZUS had a different tilt from the US one. By having close defense cooperation with the United States in ANZUS asymmetrical relations, New Zealand was able to realize two important advantages. As a "special" ally it had a degree of access to a global superpower that allowed more influence on certain security issues. New Zealand also was able to "play the American card" to maintain that country's freedom of action in security and foreign policy matters with Australia.[20]

Additionally New Zealand's participation in ANZUS allowed the small country to put less money into its own defense effort. It helped complement a national objective of greater defense force self-reliance and interdependence in facing Pacific security problems. However, as Air Marshal Jamieson appropriately noted, New Zealanders deluded themselves if they thought their nation was capable of complete self-reliance in defense. The nation's security, whether in or out of ANZUS, was still bound up with global security and the wider community of nations with whom it had trade and interaction.[21]

Lastly, before discussing a setting of New Zealand defense features outside ANZUS in the pre-Lange government years, it is necessary to place into proper context the country's two professional communities that contributed the most and received the greatest number of benefits from a full-house ANZUS: the military and intelligence communities. Subsequent New Zealand Labour government policies and fallout from

ANZUS punished principally these communities and virtually no others.[22]

ANZUS Aside

New Zealand's defense features with ANZUS aside from the early 1950s to the early 1980s had three main aspects: a continuing British connection, several assistance programs in the South Pacific region, and close cooperation with Australia. All three were overshadowed by defense policies which revealed limited independent capabilities, excessive reliance on a larger ally, and few clear-cut objectives outside of support to ANZUS.

Although Great Britain's presence was considerably diminished, part of the directed thrust of New Zealand (and Australian) security efforts in the 1950s and 1960s still went toward supporting that presence. One task, related to the slow process of decolonization and the establishment of a viable independent government, was the defeat of Communist insurgents on the Malay Peninsula. Another task was the containment of the "confrontation" of Malaysia by Indonesia. Both New Zealand and Australia had significant defense force commitments. For instance, at the height of confrontation, New Zealand had 3,000 servicemen, from all services, committed to the support of Malaysia.

One lasting low-key reminder of the former British presence was the Five Power Defence Arrangement (FPDA). Irreverently dubbed the "five horsepower arrangement" by an Australian high commissioner, FPDA gave the most advantages to Malaysia and Singapore, enabling them to build their own defense capabilities while strengthening the economies needed for effective security maintenance.[23]

The New Zealand Army, partly in response to the requirement for continued stationing of an ANZUK (Australia, New Zealand, and United Kingdom) force in Singapore and Malaysia, kept a battalion in Singapore at considerable cost to New Zealand. British forces withdrew by 1974 and most of the Australian ground contingent did the same. Called the New Zealand Force Southeast Asia (NZFORSEA), the New Zealand unit was the 1st Battalion, Royal New Zealand Infantry Regiment. Numbering more than 700 troops it performed several functions, including being a positive demonstration of external support to a once unsettled area. Singapore and Malaysia found some comfort in a shadow linkage to the United States by way of New Zealand and Australian military presence in the region. This was especially important in the first years after the mid-1970s withdrawal of American ground combat forces from Southeast Asia. As far as New Zealand was concerned, despite the expense, NZFORSEA service assisted their small army's volunteer recruiting and eased the problem of accommodating the battalion personnel (and their dependents) back home in New Zealand.

There have been few other long-term overseas involvements of the NZDF in peacetime. The most obvious recent example was the New Zealand contingent to the multinational force of observers (MFO) in the Sinai. As mentioned in the previous chapter, New Zealand integrated its helicopters and personnel with a larger Australian air force unit in a Middle East peacekeeping operation that lasted more than four years.[24]

New Zealand maintained a fairly active series of mutual assistance defense programs directed at both selected South Pacific nations and members of the Association of Southeast Asian Nations (ASEAN). These programs consisted of bilateral agreements with Malaysia and Singapore (under the FPDA), Indonesia, Thailand, the Philippines, Papua New Guinea, Fiji, and Tonga. Recently there has been a gradual shift in emphasis to the South Pacific area of more direct strategic concern to New Zealand. Types of activities there included provision of training facilities, personnel exchanges, and joint exercises. New Zealand used defense force assets to provide natural disaster relief and assistance to those countries throughout the region in times of need.[25]

A very significant feature of NZDF outside ANZUS was the trans-Tasman Sea relationship with the Australian Defence Force (ADF). There were differences in orientation, such as Australia's closeness to the Asian mainland, Indonesia, and the Indian Ocean in contrast to New Zealand's more pronounced orientation toward the South Pacific. Nevertheless, much of New Zealand's defense was predicated on an integrated response with Australia to any external threat.[26] As Prime Minister David Lange carefully wrote in a 1985 article,

> If Australian forces were engaged in combat in defence of Australian interests
> it is almost unthinkable that New Zealand defence forces would not assist,
> whether or not New Zealand interests were directly involved.[27]

This was an important point emphasizing how the Australian-New Zealand connection, at least defense-wise, was strong during times of stress. Even though each country had its own orientation and wanted to be independent and self-reliant in a qualified sense, the bonds between their armed forces, forged in wartime, had an important influence on political decisions concerning security in peacetime.

The 1944 Australia-New Zealand agreement, also called the ANZAC pact, was still used in the mid-1980s by some to justify the bilateral defense relationship outside of ANZUS. Political management was formalized in the 1970s by the establishment of such annual meetings as the Australia-New Zealand Consultative Committee on Defence Cooperation (ANZCCDC) and the Australia-New Zealand Defence Policy Group. The ANZAC relationship built up long-standing arrangements between the two close allies for training, exercising, exchanges, technical cooperation, logistics support, and intelligence-sharing.[28] Overall, the bilateral defense relationship was useful to both, especially to New Zealand. Yet the security problems between the United States and New Zealand that began in the 1970s and intensified to a "crisis" point in the mid-1980s also strained and created tension between Australia and New Zealand.

Turning Points in Defense Emphasis

Several turning points changed the traditional approach New Zealanders took on defense issues. One was the antinuclear attitude that has become so prevalent in New Zealand society today. While the foundations for the antinuclear movement go back to the 1950s, a turning point really began in the early 1970s during the third Labour government of Norman Kirk and Sir Wallace Rowling. The "nuclear" issue then dealt with attempts to make the entire South Pacific a nuclear weapons free zone. The New Zealand Labour Party (NZLP) mainstream's principal target for the antinuclear push was France, due to its active program of nuclear weapons testing in French Polynesia, and not the United States with its nuclear-powered and nuclear-capable navy. But left-wing fringes of the NZLP long had been vocal on all aspects of the nuclear issue. Consequently, these more extreme political groups extended their protests to include New Zealand withdrawal from military alliances with any nuclear power—which meant ANZUS and the United States.

When David Lange's fourth Labour government entered office in 1984, his "conservative" handling of the national economy meant some concessions to leftist NZLP elements were necessary if he wanted their support. So Lange gave them much of the foreign policy they wanted. That is one reason the subsequent port ban on nuclear ships became for political reasons "nonnegotiable." [29]

Prime Minister Lange was quick to point out that the nuclear ship ban policy was antinuclear only and not anti-ANZUS or anti-American. New Zealand has always been committed to the ANZUS alliance. But as Ambassador Rowling stated to a US congressional subcommittee in 1985, the NZLP interpreted the alliance to be a conventional defense partnership, not a nuclear one. Thus, the party saw no need for the United States to send nuclear-propelled or nuclear-armed vessels and aircraft to New Zealand.[30] Lange did not believe a positive antinuclear attitude equated to negative feelings against the United States. In his words, "Anti-Americanism is not popular in New Zealand . . . [It] simply doesn't catch on." [31]

Close connections with the South Pacific Nuclear Free Zone (SPNFZ) treaty further strengthened antinuclear feelings in New Zealand. Both Australia and New Zealand saw SPNFZ as important and necessary. The fact that the United States did not sign the protocols meant to many New Zealanders that America was supporting French nuclear policy and that the Soviet Union (which agreed to protocol parts) was the major global power pursuing regional peace. The entire SPNFZ issue soon transcended politics and became very emotional and perhaps oversensationalized.[32]

While antinuclear sentiment is now reflected among all New Zealand political parties, many observers believe that it was former Prime Minister Robert Muldoon of the National Party who politicized the issue in the late 1970s. Muldoon's government hosted several US nuclear-powered ship visits. Media attention on the protests and disturbances during the visits created a situation which Muldoon neither satisfactorily explained nor justified. His actions and comments in fact boosted the momentum of growing antinuclear attitudes. At the 1981 NZLP conference, leaders set a policy which directed that the "next Labour Government, in accordance with its desire to promote a SPNFZ, continue to oppose visits by nuclear-powered and nuclear weapon-carrying craft."[33] At the same time NZLP continued to pass resolutions calling for withdrawal from ANZUS. These were the types of major political issues on which David Lange sought middle-ground consensus when he became the NZLP leader in February 1983. Once elected, Lange found that the majority of his people remained committed to an antinuclear stance.[34]

Another turning point for the NZDF was the need to be more self-reliant and to have an independent capability to satisfy defense needs in the South Pacific region. Vietnam War involvement and subsequent disillusionment were critical early catalysts in leading many New Zealanders away from the role of a "faithful and unthinking ally" to a greater power.

Lange himself was one of the early protesters against the war. In July 1964 the young law student made his first public speech against involvement in Vietnam. His political activism then must have come to the attention of American authorities. Upon completing his law degree and preparing to embark for several years of legal work in Great Britain, Lange was refused an American visa when he requested travel through the United States.[35]

The post-Vietnam War period saw a continuation of New Zealand's defense efforts to be more self-reliant. In December 1983 the conservative government of Muldoon published *Defence Review*, a white paper that proposed restructuring the NZDF to be more self-reliant and planned for a wider role in the South Pacific. As listed in the *Defence Review*, the official defense policy objectives were to:

- preserve security and integrity of New Zealand and its 200 nautical-mile exclusive economic zone;

- promote security and stable development in South Pacific by providing, on request, practical assistance in defense matters to countries of the region;

- be able to respond militarily to low-level emergencies within South Pacific;

- maintain and strengthen defense relationships with ANZUS partners;

- develop further defense cooperation with Australia; and

- demonstrate commitment to maintain peace and stability in Southeast Asia.[36]

Additionally the *Defence Review* identified a South Pacific regional role for the army by creating a ready reaction force as well as maintaining an ongoing force structure capable of expansion in case of need. It also highlighted a need for another maritime surveillance aircraft.[37]

The *Defence Review* was a forward-looking document based on close association with partners in a functioning ANZUS alliance. Yet even before the government changed and a new shift in defense policy emerged, the 1983 white paper had a fundamental problem. Increased self-reliance required a greater budget allocation for defense, and this was not evident in the early 1980s.

The final major turning point concerned these economic circumstances. For years, effective deterrence provided by collective security allowed progressive New Zealand governments, regardless of party, to capitalize on external ties and keep defense expenditures to a minimum. Only in fiscal year 1981-82 did defense expenditures exceed 2 percent of the gross national product (GNP)—and that was for the first time since FY 1970. By comparison Australia spent almost 3 percent and the United States almost 8 percent of their respective GNPs on defense.[38] Successive New Zealand governments, faced with domestic economic problems, deferred numerous defense equipment purchases. The 1984 devaluation by 22 percent of the New Zealand dollar against international currencies created a further problem, especially since more than 80 percent of NZDF equipment came from overseas sources.

The economic situation has become more serious, in light of the general agreement that the NZDF's primary emphasis is maritime defense. Past governments were willing to purchase and maintain capital equipment in this area. Unfortunately, primary assets, especially those belonging to the navy, are fast approaching the obsolescence stage and require replacement. Yet such items are expensive, and the annual NZDF budget for capital expenditures is limited to only about 15 percent, divided among all three service components.[39]

The country's budget problems neither started nor ended with the NZDF. The New Zealand foreign debt is more than US $11 billion, one of the world's largest for a nation that size. Although unemployment in 1970 was almost zero, it had grown to nearly 6 percent by the mid-1980s. Annual inflation rates have varied in recent years but hovered around 6 percent at the time of Lange's election in 1984. The current split with the United States is costing the New Zealand defense budget an estimated extra $NZ 50 million per year. Yet New Zealand still planned to budget a scarce $1 billion on defense in FY 1986. This caused one former NZDF chief to lament, "We can do no less if we wish to maintain any real combat capability of our own."[40] Unknown is where the peacetime defense allocations fit into an already strained national budget. These problems are not new; they have been avoided or pushed aside by former governments. The Lange government's top priority was a major economic restructuring of New Zealand to a more market-based economy to help correct its financial woes. Just how the long-term increased allocations for defense self-reliance in an antinuclear atmosphere are supposed to fit in is anyone's guess.[41]

Lange Labour Government Setting

The election of the fourth Labour government headed by David Lange in July 1984 marked a visible change in New Zealand's official defense policy and relationship in ANZUS. The rapid ascent of Lange onto the national scene represented a shift in New Zealand's defense and foreign relations. Perhaps the meaning of this change was best shown in the statements issued by Lange and US Secretary of State George P. Shultz, who coincidentally was in Wellington, New Zealand, to attend the annual ANZUS Council meeting taking place at the same time as that country's federal election.

The new Prime Minister-designate Lange met privately with Shultz for a 40-minute discussion. After that meeting Lange announced that New Zealand's ties with the United States were "a very basic part of . . . our heritage" and cited his nation's "huge dependency" on the American market for its trade. Yet at the same time he stated an often-repeated theme that "it is simply inconceivable to me" that the military strategy of the United States and its allies "would be frustrated" by banning US Navy warship visits to New Zealand ports. Lange furthered the cause of antinuclear righteousness by proclaiming that it was a "very significant concern within New Zealand that we ought not be seen to be buying into a nuclear defensive capacity. . . . People in this country are saying in increasing numbers they don't want to be defended by nuclear weapons."[42]

For his part Shultz made a concerted effort to remain calm, collected, and reasonable with Lange. It was then still possible to hope that Lange's pronouncements reflected more the euphoria of political victory than deep-seated and unswerving convictions. Shultz emphasized the importance of port calls to the Western alliance. He asked rhetorically, "What kind of alliance is it if military forces are not able to be in concert with one another?"[43]

The above statements set in motion a series of official events highlighted by quiet, eleventh-hour, behind-the-scenes negotiations that attempted to break the growing deadlock between the close allies. The issue came to a head in February 1985 with the banning of the USS *Buchanan* from New Zealand. The American reaction was uncharacteristically strong and swift against New Zealand. To avoid New Zealand's antinuclear stance starting a trend which other countries might follow, the United States suspended its security guarantee extended to New Zealand under ANZUS. As Secretary Shultz later said, "We part as friends but we part company as far as the Alliance is concerned."[44]

Lange and his following in New Zealand outwardly appeared unperturbed and proceeded to press for antinuclear policies and defense independence. Lange started the political process to create antinuclear legislation in New Zealand. He advanced this with the formal introduction in February 1987 of a bill in Parliament to ban all nuclear weapons from New Zealand, saying it would be a "real measure of arms control." Only then would there be a "willingness to replace nuclear defence with conventional defence and . . . hope of an end to the arms race." [45] Political opponents in New Zealand said the nuclear free bill as presented was the "formal opting-out legislation from the Western alliance" and the "end of ANZUS in New Zealand." Nevertheless, the bill's passage in the summer of 1987 and Labour Party's return to government in the federal elections in September 1987 culminated the process. [46]

The New Zealand Ministry of Defence maintained a consistent position in wanting independence and effective forces, whether in or out of a revised ANZUS alliance. Defence Minister Frank O'Flynn talked of New Zealand's intentions to provide means that permitted NZDF to carry out a regional role in association with neighbors (Australia primarily) but with a gradually increasing degree of self-reliance. O'Flynn admitted that a small professional armed force like New Zealand's had to maintain effective interaction with larger partners. Only in this way would there be confidence in its own defense capabilities. While this apparently became more difficult to do in light of New Zealand's strained relations with the United States and differences with Australia, the minister was publicly optimistic in the beginning that New Zealand could meet the "formidable challenges for all." [47] Soon after the 1984 NZLP election, he defined the essential interests behind New Zealand's foreign and security policies:

- a secure and prosperous South Pacific region free as far as possible from confrontation;
- sound and growing bilateral relations with Australia, United States, and Japan;
- important interests with ASEAN and the European Economic Community (EEC);
- a continued East-West balance of power to ensure secure and peaceful worldwide trading and political environments; and
- a demilitarized Antarctic continent and region not subject to political or economic dispute. [48]

Within ANZUS

Considering these political aspects, what is the status of New Zealand defense features within ANZUS in a Lange government? As expected there is very little to discuss about present New Zealand defense contributions to the alliance. It is more appropriate to mention what is no longer occurring. Most of the prior bilateral defense arrangements between the United States and New Zealand are now suspended. There are no more combined training and exercises, intelligence and surveillance support, logistics and supply support, personnel exchanges, or defense conferences and consultations.

While no one knows for sure what the long-term effects will be on the NZDF, several developments are predictable. Without the US defense connection, New Zealand's military forces, in spite of increased contacts with the Australian Defence Force, will become progressively removed from developments in modern military doctrines and procedures. To be sure, such a modern approach has only limited application to the South Pacific security environment. Yet the NZDF, to remain professional and current, requires some exposure to the latest Western defense thinking and policies to adapt them to the NZDF's own needs. New Zealand's senior military leaders were already saying in 1986 there had been a significant loss by having access closed to American tactical doctrine, particularly in maritime and antisubmarine warfare systems.[49]

In the area of logistics and supply support, the effect of the nonrenewal of the memorandum of understanding was unclear. Perhaps there will be little effect since New Zealand in the past paid cash for most of its military purchases. However, although New Zealand can buy such supplies from American sources, the procedure of doing so could be more difficult and the costs higher since the country will no longer be treated in arms sales as an ally but rather as a "friendly government." Several US congressmen wanted to punish New Zealand even more in this area. Bill Broomfield (R-Michigan) introduced a bill that would officially strip New Zealand of any preferential treatment it received in arms sales and security assistance. Had it passed, the Broomfield amendment would have ended for a long time any chance of effective defense cooperation between the two countries.[50]

The virtual elimination of official association with the United States has led to an "unofficial" reaction that affects most critically the New Zealand defense community. The US position in essence denies high-level New Zealand access to American officials in Washington. Since the former ally once enjoyed such special arrangements, it is that much harder to function without them. This factor and the others present difficult problems for the NZDF. As US Deputy Assistant Secretary of Defense for East Asia and Pacific Affairs Karl Jackson testified, loss of such access to US military and political circles means hard times for New Zealand in terms of defense force structure, modernization, sustainability, and worthwhile training. If the New Zealand government decides to provide for an adequate, self-reliant conventional defense, it has to require the New Zealand people to assume more burdensome contributions to replace those assets previously provided by the United States through the ANZUS alliance relationship.[51]

One approach New Zealand is trying in an effort to ease the loss of the defense arrangement with the United States is to increase its interaction with Australia on a bilateral basis. This became a main feature of New Zealand's defense contributions outside of ANZUS after the 1984 election period. Undeterred by finding itself in the middle, Australia continues to set priorities for its own defense features. These include a definite determination to strengthen bilateral relations with the United States, as reflected in the recent series of ministerial meetings (i.e., July 1985 in Canberra, August 1986 in San Francisco, June 1987 in Sydney, July 1988 in Washington, and November 1989 in Sydney) between the two which replaced the temporarily defunct ANZUS Council sessions. Australia still acknowledges its long-standing relationship with New Zealand. It is willing, within reason, to encourage better defense cooperation and operational compatibility in such areas as central defense planning, expanded bilateral exercises, intelligence collection, and shared security interests. But as Australian Foreign Minister Bill Hayden told Lange in December 1986, Australia is not a defense substitute for the United States and will do only what is feasible regarding an increased Australian-New Zealand defense relationship.[52]

Without ANZUS

ANZUS aside, New Zealand has a strong regional relationship with the islands of the South Pacific. The Labour government emphasizes the importance of New Zealand's key role in furthering Western interests in the area. According to Graham Ansell, the New Zealand high commissioner for Australia, his government understands the "Pacific way" of the islands. New Zealand wants to gear its economic assistance and defense cooperation programs in a South Pacific context to give the appearance that it already has an impressive understanding of and is more influential than the United States and even Australia at times.[53]

New Zealand leaders also have attempted to convince their own citizens and others that New Zealand's national interests are well along in the focus shift from a provision of forces to larger allied formations far away to a more self-reliant capability directed toward the South Pacific region. They point to several ongoing and proposed developments to support such a line of thinking. New Zealand already has extensive links through its military assistance program—the defense equivalent to civil aid—with Fiji, Papua New Guinea, Tonga, Western Samoa, and the Solomon Islands (more than $NZ 68 million in 1986-87). New Zealand has a special defense concern for the Cook Islands, Niue, and Tokelau. As part of this involvement, New Zealand in cooperation with Australia provides maritime surveillance for the region. It also holds its own joint military exercises there (Western Samoa in 1985 and the Cook Islands in 1986, with 1,000 NZDF personnel) to demonstrate in Prime Minister Lange's words, "New Zealand's firm commitment to regional security."[54]

Further evidence of the regional shift was found in Lange's December 1986 announcement that most of the NZFORSEA troops stationed in Singapore under the FPDA umbrella would return home by 1989. Singapore supposedly was "comfortable" with New Zealand's decision to transfer its token military force after a 30-year presence. The end result would be a beefed up military capability focused not even partially on Southeast Asia but mainly on the South Pacific—New Zealand's stated region of primary strategic concern.[55]

These changes in national defense policy and strategy did not occur in an atmosphere devoid of internal resistance. Lange refused to take seriously into account the experience of his senior military professionals. When he announced that a panel of independent experts would be appointed to undertake a defense review (i.e., the Corner Committee of Enquiry—to be discussed later), he turned down suggestions to include any of the 17 former defense chiefs. This was primarily due to some of the retired officers issuing a public statement on defense which called on the Labour government to abandon its antinuclear stance. Lange's reaction was to refer to this collective group of retired professionals as "geriatric generals." Defence Minister O'Flynn did little better in winning friends among the NZDF members. When he publicly called some officers "disloyal" for trying to discredit the government's defense policy, he created a political embarrassment that almost turned into a crisis. The opposition called on the prime minister to fire his minister of defence. Even though Lange did not, this incident and the prior one revealed considerable tension and turmoil within the ranks and in the public service in New Zealand.[56]

Two major implications arise from a review of the recent changes and shifts in New Zealand's defense policy outside ANZUS. The first concerns the very real negative impact on the NZDF due to the downgrading of its military relationship with the United States. The small but well-trained and professional force can easily integrate itself into larger allied formations; it cannot hope to achieve high levels of proficiency by exercising and training alone. The NZDF felt immediately the loss caused by the American cancellation of planned exercises and exchanges. For example, in 1985 the NZLP had 22 programmed exercises either canceled or restructured, resulting in approximately 6,000 man-days of training being taken away. The Royal New Zealand Navy was probably hurt the most, as it saw 106 exercise days reduced to 34 due to the ending of joint exercises involving the United States. One former NZDF chief said that lack of frequent exercises and exchanges with larger allied services would cause within five years (by about 1990) a marked decrease in the existing standards of the NZDF.

The second implication concerns the government's attempt to relieve the impact of US action by increasing defense expenditures to improve self-reliance in security matters. To give a clear signal of intent, the government announced a proposed increase in defense allocation from $NZ 761 million in 1984-85 to $NZ 900 million in fiscal year 1985 to almost $NZ 1 billion (about 550 million in US dollars) the next year. These increases appeared impressive, especially since the New Zealand government traditionally devoted less than 2 percent of its GNP to defense.

While the long-term results were unknown, many defense analysts believe that New Zealand's attempts to increase defense budgets and self-reliance will have little real effect on its security posture. In fact the likely course of events could make the worst fears come true. With ANZUS aside the NZDF will lose its recent level of proficiency in modern medium-intensity warfare and its interoperability with other Western defense forces.[57]

New Direction in Defense Objectives

The New Zealand Labour government persists in its efforts to provide a new direction in defense objectives. In a display of determination, Lange directed a complete cycle of defense review and debate to find the best defense policy and force structure required for New Zealand and regional security. At the beginning of the cycle in 1985 were the *Defence Interim Review* and the government discussion paper, *The Defence Question: A Discussion Paper Issued as Background to Public Submissions on Future New Zealand Strategic and Security Policies.* Following were several significant inquiries and studies, chief among them was an examination of the defense situation by the independent Defence Committee of Enquiry (the Corner committee). The cycle concluded with the release of a government white paper in early 1987. As the Dibb report and the subsequent defense white paper were the most important discussions on defense policies for Australia since World War II, this two-year defense review cycle was likewise for New Zealand.

Government Discussion Paper on Defense

The government's comprehensive review of defense policy began with the May 1985 *Defence Interim Review*. This preliminary document was followed in December 1985 by publication of the government discussion paper, *The Defence Question*. The latter was presented as a background to the subsequent public submissions on future New Zealand strategic and security policies.

The concept of *The Defence Question* was unique. The government rightly felt that since defense and security were everyone's concern, it was important in a democracy for these issues to be brought into the open. Consultation with the people was of fundamental importance. Therefore, the intent was for this discussion paper, as a first real step in the cycle process, to stimulate coherent debate on defense and security issues. The paper was not a statement of government policy but an attempt to set the scene for public consultation. If properly done, this would be a preparation for the new government's white paper on defense in 1987, designed to end the review cycle and officially replace the 1983 white paper. The whole purpose of the 1985 report was to raise the correct follow-on questions that the public inquiry and subsequent white paper would then seek to answer.

The discussion paper's aims were:

• to provide a framework for thinking about defense issues and a reference point for those wishing to make submissions to the Corner committee;

• to outline and invite comments on the available options;

• to attempt an analysis of the more central provisions; and

• to set out the broad thrust of the government's own defense thinking with the goal of generating focused comment.

Before the discussion paper raised some fundamental questions, the Labour government made sure that its key elements of defense policy were known. The first element was that the policy had to consider how best to provide for the defense of New Zealand. Next, New Zealand's security was linked by its South Pacific focus to stability in that region.

This in turn had linkage to wider regional and even global considerations when relevant. Third, the government intended to have greater self-reliance founded on the principle of self-help. Finally, New Zealand had to be free of nuclear weapons and not a participant in any nuclear strategy (e.g., ANZUS as a nuclear alliance) for its defense. The Labour government's nonnuclear policy thus became a basic starting point in defining the country's defense posture in the future.

The paper concluded by highlighting the following key security and defense issues for public discussion:

- kinds of defense policies appropriate to New Zealand's (nonnuclear) stance and geographical position;
- military capabilities required to uphold national interests;
- degree able to stand alone in pursuit of more independent policies;
- importance of defense cooperation, especially with Australia and South Pacific partners;
- role of NZDF in contributing to regional stability in peacetime through resource protection, civic action, and disaster relief; and
- appropriate commitment level to continuing investment in maintaining effective NZDF.[58]

Corner Report on *Defence and Security*:
What New Zealanders Want

The independent Defence Committee of Enquiry, chaired by Frank Corner, was established by the New Zealand Labour government in early 1986 to facilitate debate on defense and security issues. It was the second stage of the cyclical process of public consultation. The committee's terms of reference were:

- to receive and hear public submissions on the discussion paper, *The Defence Question*, on the future defense policy of New Zealand;
- to question groups and individuals making submissions;
- to commission polling to provide objective data on public attitudes to defense and security; and

- to prepare for Lange and his government a report, based on public hearings and poll data, which would be considered in preparation of the white paper on defense policy.[59]

Over a six-month period more than 4,100 New Zealanders provided submissions and the National Research Bureau conducted a comprehensive public opinion poll. The results underwent analysis and discussion by the four distinguished key members of the Corner Committee of Enquiry:

- Frank Corner, chairman, foreign affairs secretary (1973-80), ambassador to the United States (1967-72), permanent representative to the United Nations (1962-67);
- Maj Gen Brian M. Poananga, New Zealand Army, chief of General Staff (1978-81), high commissioner of Papua New Guinea (1974-76);
- Ms Diane Hunt, director of the Policy Research Unit, Commission for the Future (1978-79); and
- Dr Kevin Clements, senior lecturer in sociology at the University of Canterbury, director of the Quaker UN office in Geneva (1982-84), nongovernment representative with the New Zealand delegation to the Non-Proliferation Treaty Review Conference in Geneva (1985).

It was Lange's intention to choose these four people for the committee based not only on their knowledge and expertise but also on their broad range of backgrounds and differing viewpoints. By so doing he hoped the committee's conclusions would reflect a valid consensus of opinion.[60]

The Corner committee's results, published in July of 1986, were not satisfactory as far as Lange was concerned. Using the submissions, opinion poll, and other sources of information, Corner's group found the country deeply divided on defense. More than 72 percent of the community desired to be in an alliance with larger countries. Yet 73 percent, most of them the same concerned citizens, wanted their defense requirements arranged in a way that ensured New Zealand was nuclear free. According to the opinion polls, "the single most preferred defence option overall was for New Zealand to be allied to the United States and Australia but separate from any nuclear aspects." Forty-two percent wanted it. Viewing this option as not achievable, based on the government's unconditional antinuclear stance, the committee saw enhancement of the bilateral ANZUS relationship with Australia as the most promising option left open. Its bottom line was that the Lange government was wrong in having a defense and security inquiry follow, instead of precede, major policy changes (i.e., antinuclear stance and ANZUS withdrawal).

In a series of letters between Lange and Corner, both sides were unwilling to compromise. In an 18 August 1986 final letter, the prime minister thanked Corner and his committee for their work but ended by criticizing some essential points, especially those on the protracted American-New Zealand negotiations from 1984 to then. In Lange's words, "The comments on negotiating mistakes are superficial, misleading, and far outside the Committee's terms of reference." [61]

Templeton Study on *Defence and Security: What New Zealand Needs*

Partly due to the ambiguities and problems associated with the Corner report, Malcolm Templeton, director of the Institute of Policy Studies at Victoria University in Wellington and a former deputy secretary of foreign affairs, produced in October 1986 an independent study titled *Defence and Security: What New Zealand Needs*. Its terms of reference required (1) an independent commentary on the political and strategic background for a review of New Zealand's defense structure and capability; (2) a clarification of the country's role in the South Pacific; and (3) use as a possible starting point for a full examination of New Zealand's strategic and defense requirements during the rest of the century. Templeton emphasized that his study was not commissioned by the Labour government or any private organization. Since the Institute of Policy Studies received financial support on a continuing basis from a number of national government departments, including the ministries of foreign affairs and defense, Templeton's study indirectly received some support from these areas, but it was "independent of outside direction."[62]

Templeton summed up his study by stating New Zealand should work to promote its national security by:

- cultivating a growing sense of common security;
- developing mutually supportive defense and foreign policies; and
- intensifying its participation in the search for effective measures of disarmament, with special emphasis on nuclear arms.

Additionally, a closer defense relationship with Australia would operate to New Zealand's advantage, provided that the latter was seen to be doing its fair share. The sooner a greater bilateral defense with Australia became part of New Zealand's policy the better, as far as Templeton was concerned. Lange was more receptive to the conclusions of this independent study and unofficially incorporated it as a third stage of the defense cycle.[63]

Government White Paper

The white paper completed the government's review of defense policy and was set aside in Parliament in February 1987. As finally incorporated in the white paper, the government stated there were two prime reasons for its defense review. The first was the need to examine defense arrangements which took into account the Labour government's nonnegotiable policy of nuclear weapon exclusion from New Zealand and the resulting important consequences for the bilateral relationship with the United States under ANZUS. The second was the continuing requirement to adjust resources to meet defense needs.

In the white paper the central objective of the New Zealand defense policy was to preserve its security and that of the island-states for which it was responsible. The policy also focused on the need for a greater South Pacific orientation for the NZDF. The main question thus became: What is required to defend New Zealand and its regional interests?

Six fundamental issues were raised in response to the main question. The white paper contained separate sections addressed to each of the following issues:

- Against what threats must New Zealand be defended?
- What should New Zealand's security relationship be with its neighbors?
- What wider security obligations and interests does New Zealand have?
- What domestic environment factors affect its ability to meet its defense needs?
- What are the defense objectives on the basis of the strategic environment and resource limitations? and
- What military capabilities are required to meet these defense objectives?

Underlying the answers to these six key questions were two principles guiding New Zealand's defense strategy. First, the country had to exercise greater self-reliance, and, when possible, maintain the ability to meet or deter with its own resources credible threats to its security or interests. The second principle was complementary to the first. New Zealand recognized its part in an international community. Should circumstances warrant, New Zealand would work with others in collective security. The focus would still be both on Australia and especially on the South Pacific, New Zealand's area of "direct strategic concern."

The Lange government felt the white paper and the preceding review cycle represented the most fundamental change in New Zealand defense policies since World War II. Although previous white papers also stressed the need for greater emphasis on New Zealand's defense role in the South Pacific, few decisions on force structure were taken to give practical effect to this shift. According to the government, for the first time, New Zealand was adopting in formal policy terms the concept of an NZDF capability to operate independently and self-reliantly in countering low-level threats in its region of direct strategic concern. It clarified that by saying the country more probably would operate in concert with Australia. New Zealand officials, at least in some circles, were confident with its defense policies, backed up by the right resource allocations, would "place the defence of New Zealand and its interests on a secure basis for the future." [64]

While Lange and his followers hailed the white paper as being just what New Zealand and the NZDF needed, others had concerns. One worry was that New Zealand wanted to remain committed to Western global security and planned to help by maintaining peace and promoting collective security in its region. Yet protecting Western security interests in a vast region without a superpower's support (i.e., collective security using both nuclear and conventional deterrence) was an awesome task. What made it even harder were the factors of New Zealand's isolation, small population, fragile agricultural economy, limited resources, and protection by a full-time defense force of 12,500 people.

Another worry was New Zealand's requirement for a strong bilateral defense link with Australia, which reflected greater self-reliance but not full self-sufficiency. Despite the ANZUS rift, New Zealand placed paramount importance on a nondependent but substantial defense relationship with Australia. Whether Australia could fulfill this and still meet its own significant defense requirements was uncertain. What was certain was Australia's refusal to replace the United States in meeting New Zealand's defense and security needs. [65]

Perhaps the greatest concern was about the Labour government's strong control over all aspects of New Zealand defense policy. The Australian white paper of March 1987 contained encouraging signs for Western collective security in the greater Southwest Pacific region. Australia intended to meet its allied security commitments and national defense needs. Regrettably, the New Zealand white paper did not invoke the same positive feelings. There was no deviation from the government's antinuclear policies and ship bans. Unlike its Australian counterpart, the concentration was generally on defense policy issues as opposed to the NZDF capabilities and equipment requirements. Perhaps the explanation for this was the fact that the New Zealand white paper was a political document. According to informed sources in Washington, it was the first defense review to be coordinated out of the prime minister's office by a political appointee instead of a career civil servant. In the past these procedures were left to the ministries of defense and foreign affairs. While the white paper officially was called *Defence of New Zealand—Review of Defence Policy 1987*, some unofficially thought of it as "Defence of New Zealand—David Lange's Review of Defence Policy 1987." [66]

Service Capabilities (Present and Future)

Until recently the NZDF has performed well despite being limited in resources. Yet problems have begun to appear and affect the state of readiness and the generally proficient capabilities once associated with the three services. The forces are in need of upgrading and modernization to remain capable and self-reliant in the region, but such improvements are part of a slow and expensive process. One problem is common to all three NZDF services: the need to replace existing material with costly, technologically sophisticated, modern equipment. The most serious aspect of this problem deals with equipment obsolescence of several capital weapon systems.

Navy

The Royal New Zealand Navy has the most at stake in the current round of defense procurement deliberations. The naval force has only 2,600 active duty members, and a blue-water offensive capability centered on four *Leander*-class antisubmarine warfare frigates. All four vessels are due to be decommissioned for obsolescence at about the same time in the mid-1990s. Due to the long lead times required for replacing such capital assets, decisions need to be immediately made if the RNZN is going to have a frigate replacement ready to sail at the proper time. The government's decision to fund a tanker ship capable of at-sea refueling will help increase the range effectiveness of the existing frigates. If in a few years, however, there are no frigates to refuel, then the tanker acquisition would be wasteful. The government realizes that a good naval capability is basic to its stated policy of providing security and stability to a maritime South Pacific region. The unanswered question remains: How will it provide the necessary financial support to have and maintain such a capability?[67]

Air Force

The Royal New Zealand Air Force (RNZAF), with a service strength of 4,200, is a reasonably capable regional air force. Very "Americanized" in aircraft, it centers in the late-1980s on 22 A-4 Skyhawks (which replaced Canberras in 1970), and six maritime surveillance P-3 Orions. Many of the aircraft are either coming to an end in service life or have been modified and upgraded about as much as they can be. Well organized, disciplined, and professional, the RNZAF is fortunate in having quality personnel who keep the equipment in peak condition despite the aging problem. The air force maintains varying degrees of operational capabilities in five basic air roles expected in a modern air force: strike, maritime reconnaissance, transport, training, and helicopter operations. These achievements are to the RNZAF's credit since it also has to deal with the perennial basic question of "where is the money coming from?" If the RNZN loses its blue-water capability or sees it diminished in the future, the air force will have to expand and improve its maritime elements by requiring more professionals, more funding, and new or upgraded aircraft. In an air force that is beginning to lose its recognized capabilities—due to the break with the United States, inability to have valid exercises, exchanges, and so on—the issues quickly multiply in number and impact. Like the RNZN, the RNZAF faces some serious problems.[68]

Army

Compared with the navy and air force, New Zealand's army does not face the same critical problems since it does not have those kinds of major decisions on capital equipment that could affect the whole future of a small military service. However, the army cannot escape the need for a reconsideration of its role in New Zealand's revised area of strategic concern.

Two events are shaping the direction of the 5,800-man ground force. First is the impact of the gradual withdrawal of the 700-man battalion from Singapore to New Zealand, completed in the late 1980s. Second is the creation in late 1984 of an infantry battalion-sized force to be maintained at a high-readiness state to counter any low-intensity threats emerging within the South Pacific region. Called the Ready Reaction Force (RRF), it is similar to the Australian Army's Operational Deployment Force (ODF). The RRF has been given priority in the Army's portion of the defense budget for both its equipment and manpower requirements. In fact the Army's manpower level has recently increased by 300 men to bring the RRF battalion up to a full regular strength of 1,200.[69]

Defense Feature Shortfalls

Despite the government's plans to make the NZDF more self-reliant and capable in the region, the future does not look good for the once proud and professional military forces. Many believe the direction of the NZDF is downward. In a revised ANZUS era, part of this is due to the unclear roles of the forces where they are on the outside looking in, instead of the other way around. The limiting factors that already have started to affect capabilities include demoralization of personnel, lack of realistic exercising, economic and funding restrictions, and low public esteem. While the danger apparently is over in which New Zealand's economic rationalists wanted to do away completely with the defense forces, many individuals remain who want to lessen the reach and power of the NZDF in the perceived "no-threat" environment. Unless the situation is closely monitored and controlled, the concern that the NZDF faces a situation of eventual "atrophy" appears justified.[70]

Among the existing and potential defense shortfalls discussed, there are three that appear likely to assume greater importance over time. The first concerns the perennial issue of keeping skilled personnel on active duty. Absolutely essential for the NZDF, small as it is, is retention of a functioning core of true professional military officers and technicians. The defense budget allocates more than one-half of its amount (51.2 percent in 1982) to personnel. Yet pay and benefits are not the only issues. The government publicly must give high priority to correcting the serious outflow of valuable professionals from the services and to creating a desirable atmosphere in which young, enthusiastic, and bright New Zealanders will want to consider making a career in the NZDF. At the present time the perceptions within and without the military are not conducive to straightening out the serious personnel problem.

The second shortfall deals with capital equipment funding and replacements. Decisions are needed to plan and prepare for major weapon system changes, especially in the navy and air force. The government should increase its 15 percent defense allocation in this area. However, that seems unlikely due to the current political, economic, and moral climate in New Zealand.[71]

The third has to do with New Zealand's efforts to increase defense cooperation with Australia. Australia can do only so much to help New Zealand, especially since its defense relationship with the United States is considered primary while that with New Zealand is secondary under the best of circumstances. Nevertheless, by virtue of the new bilateral relationship, it is Australia, and not New Zealand, that will be in a position to dictate many of the terms of such future defense relations. Such a situation does not appear to be in New Zealand's best interests since that nation supposedly wants a degree of independent self-reliance in defense matters.[72]

New Zealand Perspectives on Defense Features

Prime Minister Lange apparently harbored few illusions about his probable impact on the superpowers. He said, "Small nations (i.e., New Zealand) are like rabbits blinded by the headlights of two onrushing cars as they inexorably go and hit each other. We have no power to stop them." [73] Even if he believed that, Lange and his Labour party at least were sure they would be able to influence events in their own country and the South Pacific region. Concerning the defense relationship with the United States, he was pushing for a credible defense posture in the context of effective military relationships with the *conventional* forces of other powers to promote global common security. If the United States acceded to that arrangement, New Zealand would accommodate. Failing that, New Zealand felt there was scope and promise in the relationships it maintained with the armed forces of other nations, particularly Australia.[74] (See appendix F.)

Although the collective voices of the active military establishment were downplayed and muffled, there were still others in New Zealand who continued to provide a much-needed alternative perspective on defense issues that rose above the political overtones. They highlighted a number of legitimate concerns. The former ANZUS connection, despite its problems, gave dimension and depth to many mutual defense interactions between the military of the three nations which went beyond that provided by the cooperative bilateral or multilateral arrangements. The trilateral structure allowed New Zealand a voice on defense issues and overcame isolationist tendencies. In the changed situation since the ANZUS demise, these problems were significant for New Zealand defense. A way to address them was to increase the level of defense expenditure to a consistent 2.5 percent gross domestic product for greater self-reliance. Additionally, many agreed, including Malcolm Templeton, that a substantial effort was promptly needed to bring American-New Zealand defense relations back to something approaching their previous normality and closeness. They believed the best place to begin was in behind-the-scenes, government-to-government exchanges and negotiations.[75]

United States Perspectives

The official US government position on the break with New Zealand and the downgrading of the ANZUS alliance was well known. At the time of New Zealand's banning of a US Navy ship from a port visit in February 1985, the US Assistant Secretary of State for the Far East and Pacific Paul D. Wolfowitz summarized the American view:

Our regional alliances are important in preventing small conflicts from even starting; and since it is from small conflicts that the greatest danger of big ones arise, these alliances are important for preserving nuclear peace.... With words, New Zealand assures us that it remains committed to ANZUS. But by its deeds, New Zealand has effectively curtailed its operational role in the alliance. A military alliance has little meaning without military co-operation, New Zealand can't have it both ways.[76]

Several years later the American perspective had not changed but was even firmer. The United States reluctantly suspended its security obligations to New Zealand and reaffirmed its conviction that access for allied ships and aircraft was essential to the effectiveness of the ANZUS alliance in particular and to global security in general. The Americans would not tolerate deviation from this well-established defense policy. New Zealand's current port access policies detracted from individual and collective capacity to resist armed attack and constituted a material breach of its obligations to the United States under Article II of the ANZUS Treaty.

The United States was upset with this downgrading of relations, especially considering New Zealand's former tradition of full and vigorous cooperation with the United States and other Western democracies. The Americans also realized that the tough issues now facing the NZDF in force structure, training, sustainability, and modernization were made even more difficult by the ongoing dispute. While Secretary of Defense Weinberger stated, "We would welcome New Zealand's return . . . anytime,"[77] the fact remained that the differences between the United States and New Zealand were far from being resolved. The differences were even more pronounced when contrasted with other official American positions, as evidenced by Weinberger's often quoted comment, "The way you keep the peace is to be strong enough through *mutual action* to deter war."[78] Meanwhile, US military members regretted especially the problems the NZDF were going through, but could do little to assist.[79]

Summary

Although by far the smallest of the three ANZUS partners, New Zealand has certainly had a substantial impact on alliance and regional affairs in recent years. Few could argue that past New Zealand contributions for collective security and regional stability inside and outside ANZUS were not proportionate and useful. The nation took seriously its responsibilities for burden-sharing, first under the British and then the Americans.

A changing political climate, influenced by sustained and encompassing antinuclear attitudes evident in New Zealand and other parts of the entire region, has greatly changed the way New Zealand approaches its security and defense needs. Driven by a committed Prime Minister David Lange and encouraged by growing popular support, the country appears to have shifted its focus forever away from the earlier—and perhaps also from the revised—ANZUS formal and informal frameworks. As firm proof of the new emphasis on self-reliance and regional conventional focus, Lange organized an extensive two-year defense debate cycle. The public review was finalized with the government's publication of a white paper on defense policy that was politicized in content and overtone. The capability and effectiveness of the once professional New Zealand Defence Forces seem to be steadily declining, despite the government's official comments and the military's efforts to control and correct them.

The next chapter covers several areas, to include general observations of the current state of affairs, assessments of what the future holds, and recommendations for some defense and policy option changes involving all three of the ANZUS countries.

Notes

1. Dalton A. West, "New Zealand Security Perspective" (paper presented at a seminar on Strategic Imperatives and Western Responses in the Pacific, Sydney, Australia, 9-12 February 1986), 188, 190.

2. Ibid.

3. Robert P. Jordan, "New Zealand: The Last Utopia," *National Geographic* 171, no. 5 (May 1987): 656-61.

4. "Defense Forces of New Zealand," *Military Balance: 1987-1988* (New York: Garden City Press, 1987), 167-68.

5. Frank O'Flynn, "Formidable Challenges for All," *New Zealand Foreign Affairs Review* 35, no. 2 (April-June 1985): 18; Jordan, 661.

6. "Section 11—Defence," *New Zealand Official Yearbook—1985* (Wellington, New Zealand: V. R. Ward, Government Printer, 1985), 328.

7. Sir D. Ewan Jamieson, "Defence Dilemmas of Small Countries in the Nuclear Age," *Pacific Defence Reporter* 13, no. 5 (November 1986): 40; Alan Burnett, "ANZUS Triangle: Defence and Security," n. p., 1978.

8. Malcolm Templeton, *Defence and Security: What New Zealand Needs* (Wellington, New Zealand: Institute of Policy Studies, Victoria University, 1986), 32.

9. Statement of Stephen J. Solarz, chairman of House Subcommittee on Asian and Pacific Affairs, in House Committee on Foreign Affairs, *United States Policy toward New Zealand and Australia and the Current State of ANZUS: Hearings before the Subcommittee on Asian and Pacific Affairs*, 99th Cong., 2d sess., 25 September 1986, 3.

10. Statement of Karl D. Jackson, deputy assistant secretary of defense for East Asia and Pacific Affairs, in House Committee on Foreign Affairs, *United States Policy toward New Zealand and Australia and the Current State of ANZUS: Hearings before the Subcommittee on Asian and Pacific Affairs*, 99th Cong., 2d sess., 25 September 1986, 2.

11. Ramesh Thakur, "New Zealand: In Search of a Defence Policy," *Asian Defence Journal*, July 1985, 54.

12. Philip Riley, draft research paper on New Zealand-American defense relations for National War College, January 1987, 19.

13. Thakur, 58; Kevin P. Clements, "New Zealand Defence Policy Challenges for the Future" (paper presented at a seminar on New Zealand Defence Policy, Institute of Policy Studies, Victoria University, Wellington, New Zealand, 9 December 1986), 7; Thomas-Durell Young, "Problems in Future New Zealand Defence Policy," n. p., December 1986, 3; Ian Templeton, "Lange Moving to Make Australia a Brother in Arms," *The Bulletin* 108, no. 5541 (21 October 1986): 110.

14. Thakur, 58; Young, 6.

15. Thomas-Durell Young, "New Zealand's Dilemmas," US Naval Institute *Proceedings* 111, no. 8 (August 1985): 54; idem, "Don't Abandon Radford-Collins," *Pacific Defence Reporter* 13, no. 3 (September 1986): 16.

16. Robert A. Brand, "Australia, New Zealand, and ANZUS," *Atlantic Community Quarterly* 22, no. 4 (Winter 1984-1985): 354; Jamieson, 41.

17. "Current Defence Policies: Background," *Background Briefs for Minister of Defence* (Wellington: New Zealand Ministry of Defence, July 1984), 5.

18. Ramesh Thakur, "A Nuclear Weapon-Free South Pacific: A New Zealand Perspective," *Pacific Affairs* 58, no. 2 (Summer 1985): 225; William Matthews, "New Zealand to Lose DoD Military Purchasing Help," *Air Force Times*, 9 March 1987, 36; P. Lewis Young, "The RNZAF: Tough Going Ahead," *Asian Defence Journal*, August 1985, 76; Brand, 354; Thomas-Durell Young, "New Zealand Air Power Requirements and Force Determinants," *Air University Review* 37, no. 3 (March-April 1986): 89.

19. "U.S.-New Zealand Disagreement on Port Access for U.S. Ships," *Department of State Bulletin* 86, no. 2114 (September 1986): 1; Ronald J. Hays, "Soviet Shadow Is Apparent in Pacific Security Setting," *San Diego Union*, 10 August 1986, 6C; Allan C. Brownfeld, "Fragility of Alliance Illustrated in New Zealand," *Washington Times*, 12 September 1984, 3C.

20. Thomas-Durell Young, "Problems in Future New Zealand Defence Policy," 3.

21. Sir D. Ewan Jamieson, "New Zealand Defence Policy: A Professional Viewpoint" (paper presented at a seminar on New Zealand Defence Policy, Institute of Policy Studies, Victoria University, Wellington, New Zealand, 9 December 1986), 3; "Current Defence Policies," 2.

22. Riley, 19.

23. Burnett, "ANZUS Triangle: Defence and Security," 10; John Henderson, "New Zealand Foreign Policy," in *New Zealand and the Pacific*, ed. Roderick Alley (Boulder, Colo.: Westview Press, 1984), 91; P. D. Hastings, "Australian Regional Defence Co-operation in the 1980s," in *Australian Defence Policy for the 1980s*, eds. Robert O'Neill and D. M. Horner (St. Lucia, Australia: University of Queensland Press, 1982), 130-31.

24. Henderson, 92; "New Zealand Force, South East Asia," *Background Briefs for Minister of Defence* (Wellington: New Zealand Ministry of Defence, July 1984), 2; Thomas-Durell Young, "New Zealand's Defense Arrangements: An Uncertain Period Ahead," *International Defense Review* 19, no. 5 (May 1986): 593; O'Flynn, 19; Robert A. Brand, "Defense Down Under: An American View," *Pacific Defence Reporter* 11, no. 12 (June 1985): 13.

25. Thomas-Durell Young, "New Zealand's Defense Arrangements," 593.

26. Henderson, 85-86.

27. Burnett, 38.

28. Ibid., 38-39; O'Flynn, 19.

29. Thomas-Durell Young, "New Zealand's Dilemmas," 55; Gwynne Dyer, "New Zealand's Pesky Nix on Nukes," *Washington Times*, 1 November 1984, 3C.

30. Thomas-Durell Young, "New Zealand Defense Policy under Labour," *Naval War College Review* 39, no. 3 (May-June 1986): 22-23.

31. Stuart Inder, "The Unsqueaky Facing up to Charles Atlas," *The Bulletin* 109, no. 5560 (10 March 1987): 35.

32. Richard D. Fisher, "Why the U.S. Must Oppose the South Pacific Nuclear Free Zone," *Backgrounder*, no. 55, Heritage Foundation, 23 December 1986, 3-5; Thakur, "A Nuclear Weapon-Free South Pacific," 232.

33. Riley, 4-5; Vernon Wright, *David Lange Prime Minister* (Wellington, New Zealand: Unwin Paperbacks, 1984), 128-31.

34. Wright, 128-31; John H. Beaglehole, "Labor's Dangerous New Course," *Pacific Defence Reporter* 12, nos. 6/7 (December 1985-January 1986): 16.

35. Wright, 49-50; Andrew Clark, "Lange Symbolism Exacerbates ANZUS Schism," *The Bulletin* 108, no. 5521 (3 June 1986): 1. (Lange liked symbolism. As a university student he gave an antiwar speech on American Independence Day. Years later he wanted to use the 6 August anniversary date of the US nuclear bombing of Hiroshima to introduce legislation to ban port visits in New Zealand by nuclear armed ships. This action caused some US officials to refer to New Zealand privately as "nonaligned" and "third world.")

36. Thomas-Durell Young, "New Zealand's Defense Arrangements," 591; idem, "New Zealand's Dilemmas," 54; "Section 11—Defence," *New Zealand Official Yearbook—1985*, 320; Beaglehole, 16.

37. Ibid.

38. Paul Dibb, *Review of Australia's Defence Capabilities: Report to the Minister for Defence* (Canberra: Australian Government Publishing Service, 1986), 162; Organization of the Joint Chiefs of Staff, *United States Military Posture for FY 1987* (Washington, D.C.: Department of Defense, Summer 1986), 14.

39. Thomas-Durell Young, "New Zealand Defense Arrangements," 593; idem, "New Zealand's Dilemmas," 51-52.

40. Ross Babbage, "The Prospects for Security Cooperation between ANZUS Allies till the Turn of the Century" (paper presented at the National Defense University Conference on Pacific Basin Security: Impact of Political and Social Change toward Year 2000, Honolulu, Hawaii, 27 February 1987), 12.

41. Ibid.; "Defense Forces of New Zealand," 167-68; Brownfeld, 3C; Riley, 26; Jamieson, 41.

42. "New Zealand's New Leader Reiterates Labor Party's Antinuclear Stance," *Washington Post*, 20 July 1984, 28.

43. Ibid.

44. "U.S. Terminates ANZUS Treaty with New Zealand," *Atlantic Community News*, Summer 1986, 2; Thakur, "New Zealand in Search of a Defence Policy," 54; author's notes on keynote speech by Ronald J. Hays at the National Defense University Conference on Pacific Basin Security in Honolulu, Hawaii, 28 February 1987.

45. "New Zealand Parliament Asked to Ban Nuclear Arms," *Washington Times*, 13 February 1987, 9.

46. Ibid.

47. O'Flynn, 18-19.

48. Ibid.

49. Thomas-Durell Young, "New Zealand Defence Policy under Labour," 24-31; idem, "New Zealand's Dilemmas," 55; Ian Templeton, 110.

50. Thomas-Durell Young, "New Zealand Defence Policy under Labour," 26; Matthews, 36.

51. Riley, 19; Jackson, 3.

52. Jackson, 5; Beaglehole, 14-15; United States Information Service, American Embassy, Wellington, New Zealand, telegram, subject: Media Reaction, 110351Z December 1986, 1.

53. Graham Ansell, "ANZUS Stand Explained," *New Zealand Foreign Affairs Review* 35, no. 1 (January-March 1985): 49; Beaglehole, 14.

54. Babbage, 18; Ian Templeton, "Wellington Ponders Post-ANZUS Pacific Security," *The Bulletin* 108, no. 5519 (20 May 1986): 105; "Opening the Books," *Background Briefs for Minister of Defence* (Wellington: New Zealand Ministry of Defence, July 1984), 2; Dora Alves, "Sea Change in the New Pacific," *Defense & Foreign Affairs* 15, no. 6 (June 1987): 41.

55. Michael Richardson, "Labor under Pressure to Change on ANZUS," *Pacific Defence Reporter* 13, no. 9 (March 1987): 36; "Troop Withdrawal," *Washington Times*, 19 January 1987, 3(20).

56. Beaglehole, 16; Ian Templeton, "Minister at War with Generals Shoots PM's Toe," *The Bulletin* 107, no. 5505 (11 February 1986): 82; idem, "Lange Moving to Make Australia a Brother in Arms," 110. Frank O'Flynn, a Queen's Counsel with military service background in the RNZAF in World War II, had apparently had enough political life as the Labour minister of defense. He resigned his defense portfolio in mid-1987 and was replaced by Bob Tizard, a Labour member of Parliament, who had no previous military background.

57. John H. Beaglehole, "New Zealand Wants to Eat Its Cake And Have It, Too," *Pacific Defence Reporter* 11, no. 3 (September 1984): 22; idem, "Labor's Dangerous New Course," 14-15; Thomas-Durell Young, "New Zealand Defense Policies under Labour," 26-27; "New Zealand Military Says Standards Slip since U.S. Break," *New York City Tribune*, 2 October 1986, 3.

58. *The Defence Question: A Discussion Paper Issued as Background to the Public Submission on Future New Zealand Strategic and Security Policies* (Wellington, New Zealand: V. R. Ward, Government Printer, December 1985), 1-4, 21.

59. Defence Committee of Enquiry, *Defence and Security: What New Zealanders Want* (Wellington, New Zealand: V. R. Ward, Government Printer, 31 July 1986), 7.

60. *The Defence Question*, 2.

61. National Research Bureau, *Public Opinion Poll on Defence and Security: What New Zealanders Want*, annex to the report of the Defence Committee of Enquiry—The Corner Report (Wellington, New Zealand: V. R. Ward, Government Printer, July 1986), 89; *Defence and Security: What New Zealanders Want*, 73-74, addendum III, 4.

62. Malcolm Templeton, *Defence and Security: What New Zealand Needs*, 1-2, 54, 57, 60.

63. Ibid.; Ian Templeton, "Lange Moving to Make Australia a Brother in Arms," 110; Sir George Laking, "Assault on Economic Dependence," *New Zealand Financial Review*, December 1986, 7-8.

64. *Defence of New Zealand: Review of Defence Policy 1987* (Wellington, New Zealand: V. R. Ward, Government Printer, 1987), 8, 38.

65. *Defence and Security: What New Zealanders Want*, 89; *Defence and Security: What New Zealand Needs*, 73-74; David Barber, "New Zealand Takes Ambitious Tack with New Defense Policy," *Christian Science Monitor*, 30 March 1987.

66. Thomas-Durell Young, "Down Under White Paper," US Naval Institute *Proceedings* 14, no. 3 (March 1988): 141-43.

67. Brand, "Australia, New Zealand, and ANZUS," 353-54; Thomas-Durell Young, "New Zealand Defence Arrangements," 593; Beaglehole, "Labor's Dangerous New Course," 15-16; idem, "New Zealand's Defence: The Year of Debate," *Pacific Defence Reporter* 10, nos. 6/7 (December 1983-January 1984): 79.

68. Thomas-Durell Young, "New Zealand Air Power Requirements," 84, 91; P. Lewis Young, "RNZAF: Tough Going Ahead," 77-78, 81.

69. Thomas-Durell Young, "New Zealand Defence Arrangements," 591, 599; Beaglehole, "New Zealand's Defence," 81; "Troop Withdrawal," *Washington Times*, 19 January 1987, 3(20).

70. Confidential government source in Hawaii, March 1987; Alan Burnett, "ANZUS Triangle: Defence and Security," 54; Brian L. Kavanagh, *The Changing Western Alliance in the South Pacific* (Maxwell AFB, Ala.: Air University Press, 1987), 38.

71. Beaglehole, "New Zealand's Defence," 79, 82; idem, "Labor's Dangerous New Course," 15-16.

72. Thomas-Durell Young, "Problems in Future New Zealand Defence Policy," 6-10.

73. Quoted in "Big Man from a Small Place," *The Bulletin* 108, no. 5500 (7 January 1986): 58.

74. Clements, 9; Lange statement on "The Government of New Zealand's Position on Ship Visits," 13 April 1985. (See appendix F of this study.)

75. "ANZUS," *Background Briefs for Minister of Defence* (Wellington: New Zealand Ministry of Defence, July 1984), 7; Malcolm Templeton, "A Layman's Perspective" (paper presented at a seminar on New Zealand Defence Policy, Institute of Policy Studies, Victoria University, Wellington, New Zealand, 9 December 1986), 10; Jamieson, "New Zealand Defence Policy: A Professional Viewpoint," 8-9.

76. Paul D. Wolfowitz, quoted in Dora Alves, *Anti-nuclear Attitudes in New Zealand and Australia* (Washington, D.C.: National Defense University Press, 1985), 61.

77. Caspar W. Weinberger, "We Would Welcome New Zealand's Return Anytime," *Pacific Islands Monthly* 56, no. 2 (December 1985): 18-21.

78. Ibid.

79. Statement of James R. Lilley, US deputy assistant secretary of state for East Asia and Pacific Affairs, in House Committee on Foreign Affairs, *United States Policy toward New Zealand and Australia and the Current State of ANZUS: Hearings before the Subcommittee on Asian and Pacific Affairs*, 99th Cong., 2d sess., 25 September 1986, 6-15; statement of Karl D. Jackson, US deputy secretary of defense for East Asia and Pacific Affairs, in House Committee on Foreign Affairs, *United States Policy toward New Zealand and Australia and the Current State of ANZUS: Hearings before the Subcommittee on Asian and Pacific Affairs*, 99th Cong., 2d sess., 25 September 1986, 30-33.

Chapter 5

Conclusion

The US security guarantee can be restored as soon as New Zealand undertakes adequate corrective measures to restore normal port and air access and return to alliance cooperation.

—James R. Lilley, US Deputy Assistant Secretary of State for East Asia and Pacific Affairs

The alliance between Australia and the US is an evolving one. . . . We can look forward to [a] robust alliance based on mutual advantage, mutual respect, and an increasing familiarity with each other.

—F. Rawdon Dalrymple, Australian Ambassador to the United States

We are determined that New Zealand will accept its responsibilities for the security of the South Pacific . . . acting not only in New Zealand's but all the US' and broader democratic interests. . . . Certainly, in any future trilateral defence cooperation, New Zealand will be a more independent, self-reliant, and valuable partner.

—David Lange, New Zealand Prime Minister

This study has considered and discussed many questions and issues dealing with changing defense and security conditions in the South and Southwest Pacific regions. Although its main purpose was not to provide recommendations for governmental decisions and policy changes, it has presented enough facts and supporting information to allow for considerable observations and assessments. They in turn suggest for the three countries concerned some areas for significant improvement in actions and policies. All of these relate in some way to explaining and answering the original research question posed in the introductory section: What effects do the recent shifts in Australian and New Zealand defense features and security conditions have on those countries, the United States, and the region in the revised ANZUS era?

Summary of Shifts

The defense features and security conditions of the ANZUS showcase alliance and each of the partners have changed. Reflecting the American political leadership's view of the basic Western connections, President Reagan said several years ago, "Our ties [with Australia and New Zealand] are a precious tradition, reflecting our many concerns and shared values."[1] Today, the ANZUS organization continues to provide a modified framework for such "ties" and allied cooperation in that particular region of the world, current differences with New Zealand's Labour government notwithstanding. Yet the current differences are some of the main reasons the regional problems are growing. In addition, there remains the constant worry felt by many Australians and New Zealanders as to what extent US defense forces are really committed to protect regional security. Despite American leaders' statements to the contrary, many believe that a general lack of real concern still exists in the United States for issues relating to the region.[2] Whether justified or not, this perception—when added to the significantly altered defense features and security conditions and the increasing range of security-destabilizing factors—indicates a once secure region undergoing important shifts.

The United States is determined and committed to have a role in the Pacific and to be a great Pacific power. When it comes to providing military resources to the East Asia-Pacific region, the United States supports a defense strategy based on forward-deployed American forces, robust alliances, and self-sufficient nations with shared values and objectives. Because of the common interest among the United States and its East Asia-Pacific allies and friends in promoting peace and stability in the region, close defense cooperation and collective security arrangements are essential. However, like it or not, American defense assets are stretched thin. This point is particularly relevant for the nuclear US Navy, since the vast region is so maritime in nature. That is why a full-house ANZUS, or something similar to it and with all partners assuming a fair and proportionate share of the defense burden, is so important and necessary for the South and Southwest Pacific regions.

Since many past defense practices no longer apply in this larger combined region, an obvious need for some sort of appropriate readjustment exists. The earlier willingness on the part of the Americans to let Australia and New Zealand provide most of the military presence in the region now appears unworkable and impractical.

As US Navy Adm William J. Crowe has said so often, "The US cannot, and should not, go it alone in the Asia and Pacific theater."[3] Virtually no defense cooperation is now present between the United States and New Zealand. The result is increased bilateral cooperation between the United States and Australia to make up for the loss of the third ally's participation and to demonstrate continued strength and collective security, albeit with a different perspective. Yet it is unclear how much more extensive the US-Australian cooperative efforts can or should be. The question here becomes three-pronged for America. Are US objectives really complementary and achievable in wanting to show a greater interest in the region, pursue closer cooperative defense links with Australia, and encourage Australia to take greater responsibility for regional security? Whether ANZUS will continue to function as an operative alliance structure in these matters is still unknown.

Impact Assessments

Australia is the principal country on which will fall much of the defense responsibility for keeping the region stable. The present government in Canberra, and presumably any future one, appears willing to accept that leadership role. This position is in line with Australian policy to have a middle-power role in its region of strategic concern, which in turn allows it to make a positive contribution to Western global security. Australia is realistic in its position as a relatively small but close ally of the superpower United States. In its evolving security alliance relationship with America, Australia plans to continue having an independent partner's say and influence. An important US concern is whether Australia's changing or new-look defense features can satisfy Australian, American, and other security objectives in the region.

The Australian government's white paper, *The Defence of Australia 1987*, is the current document that indicates future direction in Australian defense policy. For the Americans it is an important and satisfactory analysis and statement of Australian defense capabilities, requirements, and objectives in a Western security context. This white paper does much to ease US worries which were evident with the "strategy of denial" concept advocated in Paul Dibb's 1986 *Review of Australia's Defence Capabilities*. While incorporating many parts of the Dibb report, the white paper still adjusts its emphasis to demonstrate a resolve to contribute to the general Western security position.

A serious factor that remains incalculable and thus unclear is how well Australia will manage its intended self-reliance improvements. The country plans to require large amounts of constant national funds for an economic structure beset by financial problems and other pressing demands. Additionally, there must be a political will, backed up by public support, to see these many developments realized. The United States has an important interest in helping Australia have the necessary defense features to be the dominant Western force in the region. Yet America is limited by its resources, defense priorities, and other obligations. Therefore, what Australia accomplishes now and in the future requires both a strong and flexible relationship with the United States and, perhaps, a greater degree of self-improvement. Though well worth the expense and effort, fulfillment of this objective certainly will not be easy.

This security ambition will require Australia to contribute on a lasting and balanced basis even more than it is now doing for defense and security matters. In spite of problems such as lack of adequate funding and military personnel departures, extensive optimism and support remain for the changing Australian defense features. The Australian Defence Force (ADF) has the ability to improve on what is already a credible, capable, and professional military force. Within limits, Australian defense policy is forward looking and will make that country a significant force in an overlapping region. Greater self-reliance and concurrent close alliance with the United States are essential features of this policy.

Unfortunately, a similar positive outlook is not applicable for the defense feature changes underway or likely to occur in New Zealand. Unlike its Australian counterpart, the 1987 New Zealand white paper focuses generally on the single issue of defense policy and does not address in depth the equally important issues of military capabilities and equipment requirements of the New Zealand Defence Forces (NZDF).

The New Zealand white paper is a very political statement that reflects the influence of Prime Minister David Lange and some of the more forceful antinuclear policy members in and around the ruling Labour government. To its credit, the white paper rightfully concentrates on the need for a greater and more effective South Pacific orientation for the NZDF. Such reasoning is sensible as New Zealand wants to achieve a degree of defense self-reliance, the South Pacific is its area of direct strategic concern, and its contributions there are necessary for Western security in that region. However, the political overtones and antinuclear sentiments of the government in power appear likely to override its stated objective to have and maintain a changed but capable small power, medium technology, conventional defense posture and force.

The New Zealand Labour government remains firm in its stance that ANZUS is not a nuclear alliance but a conventional one. It feels its antinuclear policies are not anti-American in any way. Consequently, the resulting dispute, impasse, and "bashing" by the United States are considered excessive by the standards of many New Zealanders (and others in the Pacific region). According to Lange, once the story is told of how hard New Zealand worked for a settlement with the United States on the issues under contention, many will be less critical of the former ally's actions. He also points out that it was the United States, and not New Zealand, that called a halt to efforts to reach an acceptable accommodation.[4]

Regardless of who did what in recent diplomatic discussions, the end result appears harmful not only for the once proud NZDF but also for another security-related national asset: the New Zealand intelligence

141

community. Both are hurting in regards to resources, information, equipment, capabilities, and perhaps most important, skilled professionals. When security forces are relatively small, like the NZDF, the loss of good, qualified personnel is really felt. There is no cushion or room to absorb some of the departures.

The NZDF is beginning to suffer, and the trend indicates further decline is on the way. Despite the effort to increase defense cooperation with Australia, political and economic constraints limit this practical approach. Senior leaders in the NZDF, the ADF, and the US military are worried that any real drop in New Zealand defense capability and effectiveness could soon start to have serious and lasting negative impact. The downhill slide could become either permanent or very difficult (and expensive) to correct.

Suggestions for Policy-Option Improvements

When weighing the possibilities for future regional stability and security enhancement, one must think about what is or is not occurring in the South and Southwest Pacific. Fortunately for the United States, and especially the US Navy, the "Kiwi disease" of antinuclear fervor and actions has not yet effectively spread to other areas. But the antinuclear issue is far from over. New Zealand has finally passed its legislation into law. The South Pacific Nuclear Free Zone Treaty is still on the political agenda of many regional countries, including New Zealand and Australia. Although Australia officially disagrees now with New Zealand on its nuclear ship ban policy and agrees with the United States, this loyal ally could also one day assume a much greater antinuclear stance. For many Australians from a number of diverse backgrounds, the root causes of nuclear discontent remain unresolved.

The once venerable ANZUS alliance has been substantially modified. There continues to be strong US-Australian and satisfactory Australian-New Zealand bilateral defense relations, but the US-New Zealand defense cooperation link and the trilateral relationship are gone. If some sort of alliance accommodation occurs in the future and ANZUS becomes an operative full-house alliance again, it surely will not be a carbon copy of the effective arrangement that existed before.

Policy changes that could turn around negative aspects of Western security in the region are still possible. Demonstrable and workable improvements take several forms. One form requires the three ANZUS partners, represented by their political and diplomatic leaders, to reconvene their former trilateral negotiating arrangement at least once more to adjust policy and change the existing ANZUS Treaty. While a great amount of valuable time has already passed since the last get-together, it does not make sense for the Americans to delay in the hope of working with new political decisionmakers in Australia and New Zealand, since labor governments in both countries will be in power for several more years. Thus, the American leadership should undertake some sort of positive initiative as soon as possible.

How would the existing treaty be changed? The best way would be to consolidate treaty provisions to eliminate doubt and make a contractual arrangement among the members. The goal would be either to get rid of or at least acceptably compromise contentious issues. One issue would be the vagueness of the American security guarantee to come to the aid of the others and vice versa. More tangible evidence is needed of solid intent, realistic capability, and binding criteria for assistance as they affect all three countries.

Another irritant is port access. While the US Navy is entirely correct in advocating its policy of neither confirming nor denying regarding nuclear-capable ships, surely some flexibility is possible here. After all New Zealand was a rarity for US foreign relations in that it was a true, close, and trusted ally—until just a few years ago. Since the occasional American naval port calls to New Zealand were not that advantageous and were usually out of the way, the solution appears to lie in avoidance rather than confrontation during peacetime. Only during times of increased tensions or actual hostilities involving all three countries would the United States plan ship visits. New Zealand would be obligated under such circumstances to accept the ships in accordance with appropriate treaty provisions. As long as peacetime port calls are still available in more strategically located Australia, this revised position seems suitable.

The joint defense facilities in Australia need to remain functional and in place. The United States should continue operating them on an acceptable and open basis with the host Australians. At all costs these facilities should not become bargaining chips in political and economic differences.[5]

New Zealand

To be effective, any defense arrangement, whether conventional or nuclear, must be a two-way street. If a member is not sharing the burden fairly and shows no signs of changing its ways, then that member should leave that particular defense grouping, which would mean New Zealand should depart the wide-ranging alliance of ANZUS.

Yet New Zealand, by far the smallest and most narrowly focused of the three partners and now on the outside, still has a role to play—on the inside. Past performances offer proof and current regional security disturbances provide justification. New Zealand appears to be backed into a corner from which it cannot or will not emerge. As long as its political leaders insist on having the final say on these issues, the country's defense and intelligence forces are going to suffer. The expected end result, if the present course of events continues, will be advantageous to no one.

To correct this, New Zealand can improve its defense conditions and satisfy its security requirements in several ways. First, the national politicians—especially the prime and defense ministers—must listen to and heed the advice of their senior military and defense officials. Better balanced and more appropriate long-range defense policy and objectives will follow.

Second, a realistic approach to regional security issues is vital. Fundamental to this is an acceptance and understanding that the United States is neither the source of nor savior for all security problems. However, working closely with or alongside the Americans in a Western-oriented collective arrangement is better than being opposed or neutral.

Third, the country should not expect too much from Australia under the present conditions. Their bilateral defense relations have some promise in a capacity as complementary support but not as a substitute for previous arrangements, like those found mostly within a full-house ANZUS.

Fourth, a suitable gesture of value and a desire for improved defense relations are needed. The most visible way, with the biggest impact, would be a repeal of the recently passed antinuclear legislation. While the basic components of governmental antinuclear policy will not go away—and the Americans need to realize and accept them for what they are—the symbolic removal of the law should do much to improve Australian and American receptiveness to compromise.

Finally, if New Zealand does repeal the antinuclear law, it should quickly yet quietly adopt a low profile, try to keep the defense forces' capabilities from falling further, and wait for the other ANZUS partners to act.

Australia

Australia has a pivotal role in these policy-option improvements. That role is consistent with Australian wishes to have more security influence in their areas of strategic concern and proportionate importance in the greater Western security network.

Two arrangements are possible. If an operative full-house ANZUS returns in some revitalized form, Australia should have an increased central position. Going along with the added benefits will be greater responsibilities and obligations. On the other hand, if the ANZUS alliance ceases to exist, Australia should have a lead in pushing for stronger bilateral defense relations between America-Australia and Australia-New Zealand. The middle power will then need to function effectively as a defense-related bridge between the two smaller and revised security arrangements.

In addition Australia should continue its unique defense policy objective of greater self-reliance combined with support from the United States. Proper and sustained political and economic backing are critical for success in these areas. Australian leaders accept these responsibilities, professional military members want them, and the general public must be willing to support these and related efforts. Though Australia will not be able to have all it wants, do everything it needs, and accomplish them all on time, the defense future is reasonably bright. What remains essential is Australia's ability to keep its defense objectives and policies steady and on track.

United States

While New Zealand still can have a productive security role and Australia needs to increase its value as a pivotal force, the United States has probably the primary role in seeing that these positive policy improvements occur. Such progress will take several forms.

First, the United States and Australia need to strive for even closer defense cooperation and security-related diplomatic coordination. This process, already well under way, has to go on whether in or out of an ANZUS structure. The United States, while benefiting some from the cross flow, must plan to continue providing the majority of the logistics and intelligence support that went into the former ANZUS arrangement.

Second, at the same time the United States must be willing to follow its expressed wishes and let Australia take a leading security role in the region. Since actions speak louder than words, America must be prepared to make some allowances and move the extra distance on certain issues. The United States might have to support or at least discuss more effectively, on a basis of equality with Australia, selected security and nonsecurity issues—such as the South Pacific nuclear free zone, wheat sales, and arms control—that are very important to Australia and the region. Failure to do these things and to give adequate support might force America to bring its own security and defense forces into the region in the absence of a viable security partner. This extreme measure is not acceptable, desirable, or achievable in either the short- or long-term for the United States.

Third, the superpower must be willing to allow its other contributing partners, be it Australia alone or together again with New Zealand, to have independent voices and to disagree when necessary. Like it or not, American political leaders cannot always expect to have their way—especially in a combined region not their own but still strategically important—and have others, whether allies or friends, blindly follow. Accordingly, America has to be sincerely willing to bend a bit, become more flexible, and get closer to Australia now, and maybe to New Zealand eventually. The ultimate objective must be for the three countries to seek equal and fair partnership again in a special asymmetrical state of defense cooperation.

Fourth, America should have a more consistent and active presence in the region. This greater and more visible role does not have to be just along military lines. As the most powerful Western player, the United States must design an appropriate long-range defense policy to mesh with its own foreign, economic, and political objectives as well as with those of its friends and allies in the region. The United States has to be sensitive to the legitimate aspirations and requirements of others, including the small and vulnerable island-nations of the South Pacific community. Efforts to provide more support for regional political institutions, to increase economic assistance, and to take seriously the French nuclear testing issue should be priorities for American strategy in the region.

Fifth, the United States should examine the possibilities to reopen discussion with New Zealand on a variety of defense and security-related issues. Any further penalties or punishing of New Zealand by the United States would be excessive and should be discouraged. The defense forces and the intelligence community of that small nation are already suffering. Given time and some breathing room, New Zealand's politicians might eventually try to work out arrangements acceptable to all sides. The improved defense and security relations should outweigh the perceived losses from compromising. To avoid again the spectacle of the world watching the superpower "bash" the smaller country, these future probes should be done in a low-key manner and with patience. Australia would be an ideal mediator.

Final Comment

The South and Southwest Pacific regions are still intact and Western oriented. Past experience has shown Australia and New Zealand to be exceptionally valued security partners for the United States. The former close allies were loyal, supportive, and friendly, especially since their common bonds were forged by fighting together during World War II.

Even though Australia needs to assume a true regional leadership role, the United States ultimately retains the power and resources to bring about real change, and it needs to take timely and meaningful action to keep the relationship from further deterioration.

At relatively slight political and economic costs, the United States can still provide the critical impetus in working out acceptable security arrangements. The most important requirements for the United States, Australia, and eventually New Zealand will be full support and cooperation on an equitable burden-sharing basis and with the right degrees of defense self-reliance and independence. The security partners have worked well together in the past. Hope exists that a revised ANZUS, or some other Western-style defense relationship, will be available to guarantee that genuine South and Southwest Pacific regional security extends well into the future.

Notes

1. President Ronald Reagan, quoted in Paul D. Wolfowitz, "The ANZUS Relationship: Alliance Management," *Current Policy*, no. 592 (Washington, D.C.: Department of State, Bureau of Public Affairs, 24 June 1984), 5.

2. Brian L. Kavanagh, *The Changing Western Alliance in the South Pacific* (Maxwell AFB, Ala.: Air University Press, 1987), 27, 49, 55.

3. William J. Crowe, "No 17—The US Cannot, and Should Not, Go It Alone," *Pacific Defence Reporter* 12, no. 2 (August 1985): 11-12.

4. Report of the Defence Committee of Enquiry, *Defence and Security: What New Zealanders Want* (Wellington, New Zealand: V. R. Ward, Government Printer, 31 July 1986), addendum III, 4.

5. Kavanagh, 45-47, 54-55.

Epilogue

It has been almost 40 years since ANZUS was created and more than five years since the "showcase" alliance began to unravel. (Appendix G lists significant events from 1983 to 1987.) By 1990, the alliance had undergone major revisions and most likely would never return to its former arrangement. Based on that reality, all parties concerned should focus on how the revised alliance structure and the related defense changes for Australia, New Zealand, and the United States can adjust and continue to contribute to the important security requirements of the region and, in turn, to Western collective security.

Security must be understood to be just one of several basic elements that influence the way each country, by itself or with others, conducts foreign and domestic policies. In fact, it is the complicated and powerful interaction of politics, economics, trade, and security that drives the entire process. While one element might dominate at any given time, they all exert constant pressures, constraints, and impulses.

Defense in peacetime, especially for Australia and New Zealand, occupies the "back burners" of government policies. Whoever determines the proper ways to achieve regional stability must pay heed to the reality of where defense fits into the overall scheme of things.

Another influencing factor is the changing threat environment, both external and internal. Providing adequate defense resources to meet the threats to regional stability is a primary justification for military forces. No one can deny that the changes in the world scene that began in the late 1980s are momentous and even frightening, since their final outcomes are so unknown and unpredictable.

Such uncertainty makes life for Western defense planners and strategists difficult as they try to maintain existing military capabilities and improve in those areas most relevant for the projected needs. Although the stability of the South and Southwest Pacific regions does not appear threatened by any major power (e.g., the Soviet Union), now is not the time to relax. The unknowns about possible external threats in the future dictate that effective military forces must be capable and in being today.

Internal threats and disturbances also are present in a region once envied for its peace and stability. With the diminishing of the "Lake ANZUS" concept, there is a wide variety of destabilizing factors, both real and possible. Ethnic and racial unrest has appeared in several areas, such as Fiji, Papua New Guinea, and Indonesia. Antinuclear protests have become a way of life for many. Economic imbalances and lack of hope cause potential vulnerabilities that could upset the "Pacific way" of doing things and resolving differences.

In this regional atmosphere of change and turmoil, defense forces can impact stability and security, which will affect both the short- and long-term interests of the Western countries. The question is still relevant: What present and future effects will the recent shifts of Australian and New Zealand defense features and security conditions have on those countries, the United States, and the region in the revised ANZUS era? There is no crystal ball that will reveal the future of regional security; but we can make several observations about the direction in which Australian and New Zealand defense forces and policies appear to be heading.

As the middle power that seeks to have a greater regional role and a modified intermediary function, Australia feels both positive and negative impacts associated with the ongoing changes. On the positive side, it is trying to implement and sustain the forward-looking defense policies spelled out in the 1987 defense white paper. Through training and proper equipping, the Australian Defence Force (ADF) is perhaps better prepared than ever before in peacetime to deploy elements at short notice and then operate them effectively—whether as single service, joint, or combined forces—in limited combat conditions.

The expanded Australian-American defense arrangement, made stronger and more necessary due to the demise of the trilateral ANZUS arrangement, is in good shape. There is a genuine cooperative relationship that exhibits both flexibility and growth. A vivid example of the two allies fighting side by side was seen in the 1989 Kangaroo exercise held in northern Australia. In its largest warfighting exercise ever conducted in peacetime, Australia had more than 23,000 military members (almost one-third of the active force) participating with 2,300 Americans.[1] This type of combined operations promotes better understanding and unity among military professionals and should continue.

A step in the right direction concerning equipping issues was the long-delayed decision to proceed with the Australian and New Zealand frigate-building program (10 West German-designed ships with the option for two more). Australia will coproduce eight frigates and New Zealand two in a binational program. Major construction will take place in Australia and extensive subcontracting in New Zealand. This program will help modernize both countries' navies and cause a boost for defense industries. Additionally, a construction program for six Swedish-designed submarines (with an option for an additional two) to replace the ones now in the Australian navy will start soon. The continued development of the Australian-designed Jindalee over-the-horizon radar network for surveillance of Australia's northern approaches shows great promise.[2]

Despite these positive indicators, negative aspects make the apparently sound Australian defense program and buildup—argued consistently and well by long-serving Minister of Defence Kim Beazley—perhaps too ambitious and thus stretched out or even unachievable in certain areas.[3] Two issues stand out.

First, Australia has major budgetary and resource constraints. There is the distinct possibility that the government, still led by practical Prime Minister Bob Hawke but faced with pressing fiscal priorities and economic shortfalls, will underfund its current and future defense programs. As a result, the ADF will develop a greater capability for some limited operational roles, but at the continued expense of having a self-reliant and independent force able to conduct sustained national operations.[4]

Second, and more serious, is the high loss rate among active duty service members who leave the ADF, especially prevalent among midlevel officers, senior noncommissioned officers, and technicians (i.e., those most skilled and experienced). Manpower attrition has developed into a clear crisis. In the last four years of the 1980s, more than one-half of the ADF left the military. As Australia invests heavily in a high-technology deterrent force, the ADF is not retaining the people needed to operate and maintain it.[5]

The New Zealand Defence Forces (NZDF) have their own problems. While the new frigate build/acquisition is a positive aspect, it should be noted that the prolonged debate concerning the expense of replacing New Zealand's fleet of aging frigates is one reason the decision to build took so long. As it now stands, by the time New Zealand's navy gets its new ships in the late 1990s, its existing fleet will be obsolete.

Like the ADF, the NZDF is experiencing an excessively high loss rate of valuable personnel. Because of the NZDF's small size, the problem is felt more profoundly when good people depart the military earlier than planned.

In addition, three important consequences have resulted from the estrangement of NZDF from those of the United States. The first two consequences are related. There has been a definite loss of access to subsidized US military equipment, and so New Zealand has been forced to place greater reliance on Australia for its military equipment and military exercise needs. The third consequence has spun off from the political debate surrounding defense issues and could acquire greater influence in and out of government. Political leftist groups have been greatly encouraged to pursue their policies further by reducing defense spending and introducing more isolationist tendencies.[6]

The problems must be seen in the context of the politics and economics that occupy center stage in New Zealand life. In regards to politics, Prime Minister David Lange stepped down as leader in 1989. His controversial five-year rule was marked by a vigorous pursuit (albeit inherited from former Labour party platforms) of antinuclear policies and quarrels with Western nuclear powers, primarily the United States. He was adamant in his beliefs to the end. During a final visit as prime minister to the United States in early 1989—when he lectured at Yale University but was not invited to Washington—he was candid as usual. On whether New Zealand in its relationship with the United States might try to edge back to "business as usual," he stated, "To ensure that there is no misunderstanding I think it best to say clearly that as between the US and New Zealand the security alliance is a dead letter."[7]

Lange's replacement, Geoffrey Palmer, represents the center of the Labour party, but it is still doubtful that there will be any reassessment of the antinuclear policies and addressing of the differences between the two former allies. Antinuclear sentiment runs throughout the entire Labour party, the political opposition, and the New Zealand people, despite their expressed pro-American feelings.[8]

In the area of economics, New Zealand—a social welfare state among Western developed nations—is in the midst of a major restructuring that takes precedence over most other issues, including defense. When the Labour government assumed office in the mid-1980s, New Zealand had a small, vulnerable national economy that was oversheltered, overregulated, and living far beyond its means. In servicing its considerable domestic and overseas debt (which siphoned off almost $1 in every $10 of the gross national product), the country had undergone almost no growth. Lange and Minister of Finance Roger Douglas introduced some major long-term economic reforms which eventually should help New Zealand recover and be more competitive.[9] In the meantime, there will be only limited funds available for back-burner defense forces.

The United States remains the final player in this revised ANZUS game. Its main participants in the Reagan administration, led by Secretary of Defense Caspar Weinberger and Secretary of State George P. Shultz, are gone. The George Bush administration is a new team operating in a new era.

Paul M. Cleveland, the US ambassador to New Zealand during the main period of change and troubles (1986-89), noted in a farewell speech that now was a good time to correct past problems. "We appear to be at the end of an old and the beginning of a new international-relations era, and the times call for extensive public discussion of alternative international goals and policies," he said. Concerning a return of New Zealand to full membership in the Western partnership, Cleveland said that "further repairs will be necessary in the security area. The operative questions are largely for [New Zealand] to address." He concluded on a somewhat positive note, "Because we live together on this globe, share a strategic interest in the region, and have much in common, and because we care, we will be watching with interest how you proceed."[10]

This discussion returns to the suggested recommendations for both substantive and symbolic improvements contained in the concluding chapter. Nothing has changed. Consequently, the United States has a pivotal role in ensuring that collective security in some form exists in the South and Southwest Pacific regions. Both Australia and New Zealand need to pursue their own programs of greater defense self-reliance and increased independence. Yet, for these programs to be effective and practical, certain degrees of cooperative support, interaction, and dependence must occur between those two nations and the United States.

While the ANZUS security alliance as it was will not occur again, some other Western security arrangement should be in place. Now is the time for each country's political and military leaders to firm up the modern foundation for lasting regional stability. Given the right conditions, it not only can but must be done, and the sooner the better.

Notes

1. Kate Pound, "Aussies, Americans Test Air Tactics in Kangaroo '89," *Pacific Stars and Stripes*, 24 August 1989, 8.

2. "Industry Update," *Journal of Defense & Diplomacy* 7, no. 12 (December 1989): 5; Thomas-Durell Young, "Problems in Australia's 'Defense Revolution,'" *Contemporary Southeast Asia* 11, no. 3 (December 1989): 238.

3. P. Lewis Young, "Australian Defense Minister Emphasizes Self-Reliance and Cooperative Programs," *Armed Forces Journal International*, November 1989, 44.

4. Thomas-Durell Young, 239; Michael McKinley, "Divergence in Australia-New Zealand Security Relations," in *Security, Strategy, and Policy Responses in the Pacific Rim*, eds. Lawrence E. Grinter and Young Whan Kihl (Boulder, Colo.: Lynne Rienner Publishers, 1989), 229.

5. McKinley, 229; J. D. Stevenson, "Is the Defence Force Effective?" *Pacific Defence Reporter* 15, nos. 6/7 (December 1988-January 1989): 223.

6. P. Lewis Young, "Estrangement from US Cuts New Zealand's Defense Options," *Armed Forces Journal International*, June 1989, 52.

7. David Lange, "Calling a Dead Letter a Dead Letter," *New Zealand International Review*, July-August 1989, 26.

8. "U.S. Hopes Nuclear Policy Will Exit with Lange," *Washington Times*, 8 August 1989, 7.

9. Henry S. Albinski, "Australia and New Zealand in the 1980s," *Current History*, April 1986, 151; Jonathan Boston, "The Fourth Labour Government in New Zealand: The Economics and Politics of Liberalization," *Australian Quarterly* 59, nos. 3/4 (Spring and Summer 1987): 366-76; idem, "Tough Recovery—New Zealand," *The Economist*, 11 July 1987, 69-70.

10. Paul M. Cleveland, "U.S.-New Zealand Relations: Some Parting Observations," *Department of State Bulletin* 89, no. 2147 (June 1989): 45, 48.

APPENDIXES

Appendix A

Regional Country/Island Profiles

COUNTRY/ ISLAND	POLITICAL STATUS	POPULATION	DEFENSE FORCE SIZE
AMERICAN SAMOA	US TERRITORY	36,000	NONE
AUSTRALIA	INDEPENDENT (1901)	16,200,000	(1) 70,000 REGULARS (2) 31,000 RESERVES
COOK ISLANDS	SELF-GOVERNING STATE IN FREE ASSOCIATION WITH NEW ZEALAND	18,000	NONE (DEFENDED BY NEW ZEALAND)
FIJI	INDEPENDENT (1970)	680,000	(A) 2,700 REGULARS (B) 300 RESERVES
FRENCH POLYNESIA	FRENCH TERRITORY	160,000	NONE (DEFENDED BY FRANCE)
KIRIBATI (FORMERLY GILBERT ISLANDS)	INDEPENDENT (1979)	62,000	NONE
NEW CALEDONIA	FRENCH TERRITORY	145,000	NONE (DEFENDED BY FRANCE)
NEW ZEALAND	INDEPENDENT (1907)	3,300,000	(A) 12,500 REGULARS (B) 9,500 RESERVES (1) 3,000 REGULARS (2) 6,500 TERRITORIAL
NIUE	SELF-GOVERNING STATE IN FREE ASSOCIATION WITH NEW ZEALAND	3,000	NONE (DEFENDED BY NEW ZEALAND)
PAPUA NEW GUINEA	INDEPENDENT (1975)	3,400,000	3,200 (SOME INFORMAL DEFENSE OBLIGA- TIONS FROM AUSTRALIA)
SOLOMON ISLANDS	INDEPENDENT (1978)	250,000	NONE
TOKELAU	NEW ZEALAND TERRITORY	1,500	NONE (DEFENDED BY NEW ZEALAND)
TONGA	INDEPENDENT (1920)	100,000	SEVERAL HUNDREDS
WESTERN SAMOA	INDEPENDENT (1962)	150,000	NONE
VANUATU (FORMERLY NEW HEBRIDES)	INDEPENDENT (1980)	130,000	NONE

Source: Thomas W. Shubert, "The United States and the Southwest Pacific: Policy Options for a Changing Region" (master's thesis, Naval Postgraduate School, 1986), 23; "The Military Balance, 1985/86," *Air Force Magazine*, February 1986, 94, 101, 111.

159

Appendix B

The ANZUS Treaty

TREATY BETWEEN THE GOVERNMENTS OF NEW ZEALAND, AUSTRALIA, AND THE UNITED STATES OF AMERICA CONCERNING SECURITY

The Parties to this Treaty,

Reaffirming their faith in the purpose and principles of the Charter of the United Nations and their desire to live in peace with all peoples and all Governments, and desiring to strengthen the fabric of peace in the Pacific Area,

Noting that the United States already has arrangements pursuant to which its armed forces are stationed in the Philippines, and has armed forces and administrative responsibilities in the Ryukyus, and upon the coming into force of Japanese Peace Treaty may also station armed forces in and about Japan to assist in the preservation of peace and security in the Japan Area,

Recognizing that Australia and New Zealand as members of the British Commonwealth of Nations have military obligations outside as well as within the Pacific Area,

Desiring to declare publicly and formally their sense of unity, so that no potential aggressor could be under the illusion that any of them stand alone in the Pacific Area, and

Desiring further to coordinate their efforts for collective defence for the preservation of peace and security pending the development of a more comprehensive system of regional security in the Pacific Area,

Therefore declare and agree as follows:

Article I

The Parties undertake, as set forth in the Charter of the United Nations, to settle any international disputes in which they may be involved by peaceful means in such a manner that international peace and security and justice are not endangered and to refrain in their international relations from the threat or use of force in any manner inconsistent with the purposes of the United Nations.

Article II

In order more effectively to achieve the objective of this Treaty the Parties separately and jointly by means of continuous and effective self-help and mutual aid will maintain and develop their individual and collective capacity to resist armed attack.

Article III

The Parties will consult together whenever in the opinion of any of them the territorial integrity, political independence or security of any of the Parties is threatened in the Pacific.

Article IV

Each Party recognizes that an armed attack in the Pacific Area on any of the Parties would be dangerous to its own peace and safety and declares that it would act to meet the common danger in accordance with its constitutional processes.

Any such armed attack and all measures taken as a result thereof shall be immediately reported to the Security Council of the United Nations. Such measures shall be terminated when the Security Council has taken the measures necessary to restore and maintain international peace and security.

Article V

For the purpose of Article IV, an armed attack on any of the Parties is deemed to include an armed attack on the metropolitan territory of any of the Parties, or on the island territories under its jurisdiction in the Pacific or on its armed forces, public vessels or aircraft in the Pacific.

Article VI

This Treaty does not affect and shall not be interpreted as affecting in any way the rights and obligations of the Parties under the Charter of the United Nations or the responsibility of the United Nations for the maintenance of international peace and security.

Article VII

The parties hereby establish a Council, consisting of their Foreign Ministers or their Deputies, to consider matters concerning the implementation of this Treaty. The Council should be so organized as to be able to meet at any time.

Article VIII

Pending the development of a more comprehensive system of regional security in the Pacific Area and the development by the United Nations of more effective means to maintain international peace and security, the Council, established by Article VII, is authorized to maintain a consultative relationship with States, Regional Organizations, Associations of States or other authorities in the Pacific Area in a position to further the purposes of this Treaty and to contribute to the security of that Area.

Article IX

This Treaty shall be ratified by the Parties in accordance with their respective constitutional processes. The instruments of ratification shall be deposited as soon as possible with the Government of Australia, which will notify each of the other signatories of such deposit. The Treaty shall enter into force as soon as the ratifications of the signatories have been deposited.

Article X

This Treaty shall remain in force indefinitely. Any Party may cease to be a member of the Council established by Article VII one year after notice has been given to the Government of Australia, which will inform the Governments of the other Parties of the deposit of such notice.

Article XI

This Treaty in the English language shall be deposited in the Archives of the Government of Australia. Duly certified copies thereof will be transmitted by that Government to the Governments of each of the other signatories.

IN WITNESS WHEREOF the undersigned **Plenipotentiaries have signed this Treaty.**

DONE at the city of San Francisco this first day of September, 1951.

For Australia: PERCY C. SPENDER

For New Zealand: C.A. BERENDSEN

For the United States of America: DEAN ACHESON
                                                       JOHN FOSTER DULLES
                                                       ALEXANDER WILEY
                                                       JOHN J. SPARKMAN

Source: Dora Alves, *Anti-nuclear Attitudes in New Zealand and Australia* (Washington, D.C.: National Defense University, 1985), 67-71.

Appendix C

Defense Forces of Australia

GDP	1984/5:	$A 209.54bn		($US 162.48bn)
	1985/6:	$A 231.98bn		($US 162.36bn)
growth	1984/5:	4.4%	1985/6:	3.8%
Inflation	1985/6:	8.5%	1986:	9.8%
Debt	1985:	$US 54.3bn	1986:	$US 68.2 bn
Def budget	1985/6:	$A 6.67bn	($US 4.67bn)	
	1986/7:	$A 7.42bn	($US 4.80bn)	
$US 1 = $A	(1984/5):	1.2896	(1985/6): 1.4288	
	(1986/7):	1.5461		

$A = Australian dollars

Population: 16,428,000

	18-30	31-45
Men:	1,735,000	1,775,000
Women:	1,677,000	1,723,000

TOTAL ARMED FORCES:
Active: 70,500.
   Terms of Service: voluntary.
Reserves: 26,112.

ARMY: 32,000.
1 field force command: 7 military districts.
1 infantry division w/3 brigades (1 mechanized, 2 infantry) each 2 battalions.
1 armored regiment (3 squadrons).
1 reconnaissance regiment.
1 armored personnel carrier (APC) regiment.
3 artillery regiments (1 medium, 2 field); 1 locating battery.
1 air defense (AD) regiment; 1 light AD battery.
1 field engineer, 1 construction, 1 field survey regiments.
2 signals regiments; 6 independent squadrons.
1 Special Air Service (SAS) regiment (3 squadrons).
3 transport regiments (1 air support).

7 supply battalions.

1 independent infantry company.

Army Aviation:

    1 rgmt (2 recce, 1 command support, 1 utility sqdns).

    5 independent squadrons (plus 9 reserve).

    1 aviation school + base workshop battalion.

Logistics command HQ:

    11 transport units, 6 supply, 4 workshop battalions; 9 supply, 7 workshop
        companies.

Training command.

RESERVES include: 2 division HQs, 1 Field Force Group HQ; 4 brigade HQs; 4 recce regiments, 3 independent squadrons; 16 infantry battalions, 5 independent companies; 5 artillery regiments (4 field, 1 medium), 3 independent field batteries, 2 locating batteries; 5 engineer regiments (3 field, 2 construction); 7 signals, 9 transport squadrons; 1 cdo regiment, 2 cdo companies; 3 surveillance units.

Equipment:

Tanks: 103 *Leopard* 1A3.

AFV: MICV: 63 M-113 with 76mm gun (48 with *Scorpion*, 15 with *Saladin* turrets).

    APC: 725 M-113 (including variants).

Artillery: Howitzer: 105mm: 258; 155mm: 36 M-198.

Mortar: 81mm: 280.

ATK: RCL: 84mm: *Carl Gustav*; 106mm: 70 M-40.

ATGW: 10 *Milan*.

AD: SAM: Redeye, 20 *Rapier*, 18 RBS-70.

Aviation: Aircraft: 14 1 PC-6 *Turbo-Porter*, 13 GAF N-22B *Missionmaster*.

    Helicopter: 47 Bell 206B-1 *Kiowa*.

Marine: 16 LCM, 87 LARC-5 amphibious craft.

(On order: 105 105mm light guns, 42 RBS-70 SAM launchers; 25 2-70 helicopters).

NAVY: 15,700 (including Fleet Air Arm).

Fleet Command, Support Command, 6 Naval Area commands.

Bases: Sydney (HQ), Melbourne, Jervis Bay, Brisbane, Cairns, Darwin, Freemantle.

Submarines: 6 *Oxley* (modernized *Oberon* class).

Destroyers: 3 *Perth* (US *Adams*) ASW (being modernized) with 1 *Standard* SAM, 2 *Ikara* ASW.

Frigates: 9:

4 *Adelaide* (FFG-7) with 1 *Harpoon* SSM, 1 *Standard* SAM, 2 AS-350
     helicopters;
5 *River* with 1 x 4 *Seacat* SAM/SSM, 1 *Ikara* ASW.

Patrol craft, large: 20: 15 PCF-420 *Freemantle*, 5 *Attack* (5 Reserve training).
Minehunters: 2:
     1 modernized British *Ton* coastal;
     1 *Bay*-class inshore catamaran.
Amphibious: LCT: 6 (1 Reserve training, 3 in reserve).
Support: LSH: 1 (heavy amphibious transport ship).
     1 Fleet flagship/destroyer tender with 1 *Wessex/Sea King* helicopter.
     1 ex-ocean ferry (training/logistics support).
     1 replenishment tanker.
     3 Marine Science Force survey ships.
FLEET AIR ARM: (1,200);
     no combat aircraft, 7 armed helicopters.
     ASW: 1 helicopter squadron with 7 *Sea King* Mk 50.
     Utility/SAR: 2 squadrons:
     1 helicopter squadron with 10 *Wessex* 31 B;
     1 composite squadron with 6 Bell (3 UH-1B, 3 206B),
     6 AS-350B *Ecureuil (Squirrel)* helicopters, 2 HS-748
     Electronic Warfare training aircraft.

(On order: 2 FFG-7 frigates, 1 *Bay*-class MCM catamaran; 16 Sikorsky S-70B2
    ASW helicopters).

AIR FORCE: 22,800:
     some 148 combat aircraft, no armed helicopters.
FGA/recce: 2 squadrons with 14 F-111C, 4 F-111A, 4 RF-111C.
Interceptor/FGA: 3 squadrons with 60 *Mirage* IIIO, 12 Mirage IIID.
Maritime Recce: 2 squadrons with 20 P-3C *Orion*.
OCU: 1 squadron with some 21 F/A-18, 13 MB-326H.
Forward air control: 1 flight with 4 CA-25 *Winjeel*.
Transport: 6 squadrons:
     2 with 24 C-130E/H *Hercules*;
     1 with 4 Boeing 707-338C (to be tanker aircraft);
     2 with 20 CC-08 (DHC-4 *Caribou*);
     1 VIP with 4 BAe (2 BAC-111, 2 HS-748), 3 *Falcon* 20.
Helicopter: Transport: 1 medium helicopter squadron with 8 CH-47 *Chinook* (3
    in reserve).
     Utility: 3 helicopter squadrons with 30 UH-1B/H *Iroquois*.
     (All helicopters, except CH-47, to be transferred to Army 1987-97).
Training: 81 MB-326H (life-extended), 8 HS-748T2, 48 CT-4/4A *Airtrainer*
    aircraft, 18 AS-350 *Ecureuil* helicopters.
AAM: *Sparrow* AIM-7M, *Sidewinder* AIM-9L, -9M, *Matra* 530, -550.

ASM: AGM-84 *Harpoon*.

Air Defence: *Jindalee* OTH-B radar: 1 on trials, 4 planned.

(On order: some 54 F/A-18 FGA/interceptor/training, 67 PC-9 training aircraft, 14 S-70 helicopters).

Forces Abroad:

Malaysia/Singapore: 1 infantry company, 1 squadron with *Mirage* IIIO, and 1 flight with CC-08 aircraft.

Papua New Guinea: 135 personnel and; 1 training unit, 1 engineer unit, and 100 advisors.

Indian Ocean: 2 destroyers 1 amphibious (Headquarters Perth).

Advisers in Indonesia, Malaysia, Philippines, Singapore, Solomon Islands, Vanuatu, Fiji, Tonga, and Western Samoa.

PARA-MILITARY:

Bureau of Customs; 10 GAF N-22B *Searchmaster* maritime recce aircraft; 6 small craft.

Source: *Military Balance: 1987-1988* (New York: Garden City Press, 1987), 152-53.

Appendix D

Major Military Exercises of ANZUS Members–
Mid-1982 to Mid-1983

APPROXIMATE DATE	EXERCISE NAME	TYPE	COUNTRIES	SERVICE COMPONENTS
JULY 1982	(A) FREEDOM PENNANT	MARITIME & AMPHIBIOUS	US, AUS	NAVY, ARMY
	(B) PACIFIC RESERVE	LAND WARFARE	US, AUS	ARMY
	(C) PITCH BLACK	AIR DEFENSE	AUS	ALL SERVICES, JOINT
	(D) DIAMOND DOLLAR	AMPHIBIOUS	AUS	NAVY, ARMY, JOINT
OCTOBER 1982	(A) THERMAL GALE	SPECIAL WARFARE & COUNTER-TERRORIST	US, AUS	SPECIAL FORCES, OTHER GOVERNMENT AGENCIES
	(B) BOMB COMP	AIR WARFARE	US, AUS	AIR FORCE
	(C) RED FLAG	AIR WARFARE	US, AUS	AIR FORCE
	(D) FIVE POWER (IADS)	AIR DEFENCE	AUS, NZ, UK, MALAY-SIA, SINGA-PORE (FPDA)	AIR FORCE, NAVY
NOVEMBER 1982	(A) SAND-GROPER	MARITIME	US, AUS, NZ	AIR FORCE, ARMY
	(B) –	COMMAND & SIGNALS	US, AUS, NZ	ARMY
	(C) FIN-CASTLE TROPHY	ASW	AUS, NZ, UK, CANADA	AIR FORCE
JANUARY 1983	(A) TASMAN RESERVE	LAND WARFARE	AUS, NZ	ARMY
	(B) PACIFIC RESERVE	LAND WARFARE	US, AUS	ARMY
MARCH 1983	(A) SEA EAGLE	ASW	US, AUS, NZ	AIR FORCE, NAVY
	(B) FIVE POWER IADS	AIR DEFENSE	FPDA	AIR FORCE, NAVY
	(C) TASMAN RESERVE	LAND WARFARE	AUS, NZ	ARMY
APRIL 1983	(A) FPDA	COMMAND POST	AUS, NZ, UK, MALAYSIA, SINGAPORE	ARMY
	(B) COPY THUNDER	AIR SUPERIORITY	US, AUS, PHILLIPINES	AIR FORCE

Appendix D (continued)

APPROXIMATE DATE	EXERCISE NAME	TYPE	COUNTRIES	SERVICE COMPONENTS
	(C) ROLL CALL	MARITIME	US, AUS, NZ, UK, CANADA	NAVY
MAY 1983	(A) WANTOK WARRIOR	LAND WARFARE	AUS, PNG	ARMY
	(B) NEW HORIZON	MARITIME	AUS, INDONESIA	NAVY
	(C) PACIFIC BOND	LAND WARFARE	US, AUS	ARMY
	(D) REINDEER	LAND WARFARE	AUS, UK	ARMY
	(E) BULLSEYE	AIRLIFT	CANADA, UK	AIR FORCE
	(F) PITCH BLACK	AIR DEFENSE	AUS	ALL SERVICES, JOINT
JUNE 1983	(A) VOLANT RODEO	AIRLIFT	US, AUS	AIR FORCE
	(B) STARFISH	MARITIME	FPDA	AIR FORCE, NAVY
	(C) COBRA KING	LAND WARFARE	AUS, THAILAND	ARMY
	(D) NORTH STAR/ SOUTHERN CROSS	LAND WARFARE	AUS, UK	ARMY
	(E) TROPIC LIGHTNING	LAND WARFARE & COMMAND POST	US, AUS	ARMY
OCTOBER 1983	(A) KANGAROO	COMBINED ARMS	US, AUS, NZ	ALL SERVICES
CONTIN-UOUS	(A) EXERCISE SERIES— ANZUS RELATED TO INCLUDE US 7TH FLEET	MARITIME & AMPHIBIOUS	US, AUS	NAVY, ARMY
"	(B) EXERCISE SERIES	LAND WARFARE	AUS, MALAYSIA	ARMY
"	(C) TAMEX (5X)	ASW	US, AUS, NZ	AIR FORCE, NAVY
"	(D) WILLOH	AIR WARFARE	AUS, NZ	AIR FORCE

Sources: Defence Department, *Defence Report 1982-83* (Canberra: Australian Government Publishing Service, 1983), 13-16; Dora Alves, *The ANZUS Partners*, Georgetown University Significant Issue Series 6, no. 8 (Washington, D.C.: Center for Strategic and International Studies, 1984), 77-80.

Appendix E

Defense Forces of New Zealand

GDP	1984/85:	$NZ 40.40bn	($US 21.36bn)
	1985/86:	$NZ 44.09bn	($US 22.70bn)
growth	1985/86:	0.8%	1986/87: -0.8%
Inflation	1985:	6.3%	1986: 10.4%
Debt	1985:	$US 14.7bn	1986: $US 14.9bn
Def budget	1985/86:	$NZ 911.58m	(US$ 469.35m)
	1986/87:	$NZ 1.06bn	(US$ 560.79m)
FMA	1984:	$US 1.2m	1985: $US 1.4m
$US 1 = $NZ	(1984/85):	1.8914	(1985/86): 1.9422
	(1986/87):	1.8884	

$NZ = New Zealand dollars

Population: 3,317,000

	18-30	31-45
Men:	379,000	339,000
Women:	368,000	340,000

TOTAL ARMED FORCES:
Active: 12,600.

Terms of service: voluntary, supplemented by Territorial Army service: 7 weeks basic, 20 days per year.

Reserves: 9,352. *Regular* 2,915: Army 1,370, Navy 755, Air 790. *Territorial* 6,437: Army 5,728, Navy 489, Air 220.

ARMY: 5,800.
2 infantry battalions.

1 artillery battery.

1 light armored squadron.

1 SAS squadron.

Reserves: Territorial Army: 6 infantry battalions, 4 field, 1 medium artillery batteries, 1 recce, 1 APC, 1 ATK sqdns.

Equipment:
Tanks: light: 26 *Scorpion*.
APC: 72 M-113.
Artillery: 57: Guns: 105mm: 8 Hamel; 140mm: 10 5.5-in. Howitzer: 105mm: 39
   (including pack).
Mortar: 81mm: 74.
ATK: RL: LAW. RCL: 84mm: *Carl Gustav*; 106mm: 18 M-40.
(On order: 16 Hamel 105mm guns).

NAVY: 2,600.
Base: Auckland.
Frigates: 4 *Leander* with 1 *Wasp* helicopter:
   3 have 1 x 4 *Seacat* SAM;
   1 has 2 x 4 *Seacat*, 1 *Ikara* ASW.
Patrol craft, large: 4 *Lake*; **inshore:** 4 *Kiwi* (Reserves).
Survey vessels: 3.
Miscellaneous: 1 oceanographic vessel.
Helicopter: 7 Westland *Wasp* (see Air Force).
(On order: 1 12,300-ton tanker (1987), *Seacat* SAM).

AIR FORCE: 4,200.
   43 combat aircraft, 7 armed helicopters.
Operations Group:
   FGA: 2 squadrons with 17 A-4K, 5 TA-4K *Skyhawk*.
   MR: 1 squadron with 6 P-3K *Orion*.
   COIN: 1 with 15 BAC-167 *Strikemaster*.
   ASW helicopters: 7 *Wasp* (Navy-assigned).
   Transport: 3 squadrons:
      aircraft: 1 with 5 C-130H *Hercules*, 1 with 7 HS-748 *Andover*, 2 Boeing
         727-100C;
      helicopters: 1 with 6 *Sioux* (Bell 47), 12 Bell UH-1D/H.
   Communications: 1 flight with 3 Cessna 421C.
Support Group:
      Training: 1 wing with 4 *Airtourer*, 15 CT-4 *Airtrainer*, 3 F-27 *Friendship*
         aircraft; 3 *Sioux* helicopters.

Forces Abroad:

Singapore: 1 infantry battalion with logistics support, 1 support helicopter unit (3 UH-1); to be withdrawn.

Egypt (Sinai MFO): 35; 2 UH-1 helicopters; now withdrawn.

Source: *Military Balance: 1987-1988* (New York: Garden City Press, 1987), 167-68.

Appendix F

The Government of New Zealand's Position on Ship Visits

New Zealand Prime Minister David Lange's statement appeared in the 13 April 1985 edition of the *New Zealand Listener* magazine and is the Labour Party's view of the position of the United States and New Zealand regarding ship visits.

In the face of the New Zealand Government's determination to persist in its intention to exclude nuclear weapons, the US made a request for a port visit by a vessel which appeared to comply with New Zealand's policy. The difficulty for the New Zealand Government was that the Americans could not allow themselves to be seen to be complying with New Zealand's policy. The American defence posture requires the presentation of their vessels at any time capable of defensive action with nuclear weapons, whether or not any given vessel is at any given time nuclear armed. Whatever vessel came to New Zealand, that vessel could not, in terms of that posture, be allowed to be identified as unarmed with nuclear weapons. It was for that reason that the US had previously made plain its reservations about any proposal to legislate to exclude nuclear weapons from New Zealand waters. Any such action was incompatible with the American wish to protect the untrammelled movement of its nuclear capacity.

American reluctance to send a vessel to New Zealand which would not only be unarmed with nuclear weapons but which would be seen to be unarmed with nuclear weapons forced the New Zealand Government's hand. To accept a vessel which was the subject of American assertions as to its nuclear readiness would effectively defeat the New Zealand policy, whether or not any given vessel was nuclear armed. The only tenable position left to the New Zealand Government was to accept a vessel which it could establish from its own resources was not nuclear armed. An examination was made which could establish no more than the broad probability that a particular vessel was not nuclear armed. The possibility that nuclear weapons were present could not be conclusively eliminated, and for that reason the New Zealand Government declined the application for a port visit.

The disappointment which was felt by both sides at this point in the proceedings was understandable. The US reaction was stern. It has severely curtailed its defence and intelligence co-operation with New Zealand. While the ANZUS alliance remains formally in place, considerable questions have been raised about the structure and future direction of the New Zealand military and intelligence effort, not to mention the conduct of our international relations.

The political problems posed by the American action are acute. The National party, which has pledged to return New Zealand to "full and active membership of the ANZUS alliance," cannot do so without at the least being seen as admitting nuclear weapons to New Zealand. Such an action would satisfy some elements of opinion in New Zealand but it could not restore any kind of consensus about the ANZUS alliance. The Labour Government must accommodate the deep-seated feelings of insecurity which have been awakened by the attenuation.

Of the defence relationship with the US:

The possibility of consensus about New Zealand's defence arrangements lies in the development of a credible defence posture in the context of effective military relationships with the conventional forces of other powers. There is scope for that development within the framework of the ANZUS alliance, if the US will accede to it; failing that, there is scope in the relationships New Zealand maintains with the armed forces of other nations, Australia not least.

It is clear that the building of a consensus about New Zealand's defence and security interests will not be rapidly achieved. The element of partisanship will not be easily eliminated and will continue to obscure our common interest. It is in that interest that a careful and serious examination and assessment of New Zealand policy in defence and international relations should be made.

Source: Dora Alves, *Anti-nuclear Attitudes in New Zealand and Australia* (Washington, D.C.: National Defense University Press, 1985), 79-81.

Appendix G

Significant Event Chronology (1983-87)

Mar 1983 — Australian Labor Party (ALP), with Prime Minister Bob Hawke, won sweeping victory in Australian federal election. Eight-year Liberal/National coalition of Prime Minister Malcolm Fraser ended.

late 1983 — Australian government conducted complete review of ANZUS and expressed strong continuing support.

Dec 1983 — New Zealand white paper on defense presented (superseded 1978 review).

Jul 1984 — New Zealand Labour Party (NZLP), with Prime Minister David Lange, won federal election in New Zealand. Replaced nine-year National Party rule of Prime Minister Sir Robert Muldoon.

— Annual ANZUS Council meeting in Wellington, New Zealand, took place immediately after results of federal election. US Secretary of State George P. Shultz met with newly chosen Prime Minister Lange and stressed importance and value of the ANZUS alliance.

Aug 1984 — South Pacific Forum unanimously endorsed Australia's proposal for a South Pacific nuclear-free zone.

Oct 1984 — Background briefing papers for New Zealand Labour Minister for Defence Frank O'Flynn made available for public release.

Nov 1984 — Republican Ronald Reagan won national reelection as US president in landslide victory.

Jan 1985 — US government requested permission for conventionally powered destroyer USS *Buchanan* to visit New Zealand. New Zealand Labour government unable to reach decision.

Feb 1985 — New Zealand government officially refused USS *Buchanan* visit. ANZUS began unraveling process.

179

— Australian Prime Minister Hawke visited Washington. ALP pressure forced him to repudiate Australian government agreement to assist with US testing of MX missile.

— Australian Minister for Defence Kim Beazley commissioned academic Paul Dibb to undertake a one-year review of Australia's defense capabilities.

Apr 1985 — Memorandum of understanding (MOU) on logistics support between the United States and Australia reaffirmed (preceded by 1980 and 1965 arrangements).

May 1985 — New Zealand released its *Defence Interim Review*.

Jul 1985 — Bilateral ANZUS Council meeting with Australia and the United States (New Zealand absent) held in Canberra.

Sep 1985 — New Zealand Deputy Prime Minister Geoffrey Palmer made unsuccessful "door opening" visit to United States.

Dec 1985 — New Zealand Labour government published *The Defence Question: A Discussion Paper Issued as Background to the Public Submission on Future New Zealand Strategic and Security Policies.*

— Prime Minister Lange introduced into Parliament the New Zealand nuclear free zone, disarmament, and arms control bill.

June 1986 — Secretary of State Shultz and Prime Minister Lange met at foreign ministers meeting in Manila and parted as "friends, but no longer allies."

— Dibb's *Review of Australia's Defence Capabilities* tabled in Australian Parliament.

Aug 1986 — In place of annual ANZUS Council meeting, the United States and Australia held bilateral talks in San Francisco. The United States, following upon its ending of nearly all military cooperation with New Zealand in 1985, suspended obligation under ANZUS to assist New Zealand in event of attack.

| | — | New Zealand government published its official Corner Committee of Enquiry report, *Defence and Security: What New Zealanders Want.* |

— New Zealand government published its official Corner Committee of Enquiry report, *Defence and Security: What New Zealanders Want.*

— New Zealand defense forces on their own conducted joint military maneuvers and operations on the Cook Islands in the South Pacific.

Oct 1986 — New Zealand's unofficial Templeton study, on *Defence and Security: What New Zealand Needs,* released.

Dec 1986 — New Zealand announced that most of its overseas army battalion in Singapore will return home by 1989.

— Australian Foreign Minister Bill Hayden told Prime Minister Lange in Wellington that Australia would not be a substitute for the United States on defense matters and that increased Australian-New Zealand defense cooperation had practical limits.

Feb 1987 — New Zealand published *Defence of New Zealand—Review of Defence Policy 1987.* It superseded the 1983 white paper and was the culmination of a two-year government comprehensive defense review which began with the May 1985 *Defence Interim Review.*

— US Department of State announced that the long-standing MOU on logistics support between the United States and New Zealand (as preceded by 1982 and 1985 arrangements) would not be renewed.

Mar 1987 — Australia published its government white paper *The Defence of Australia 1987.* It superseded the 1976 white paper and incorporated many of the main points from the Dibb report and the concerns expressed by the US government.

Jun 1987 — Bilateral ministerial meeting between the United States and Australia held in Sydney. This was the third such bilateral meeting which replaced the former annual ANZUS Council meeting (with New Zealand in attendance).

— New Zealand Parliament finally passed the Nuclear-Free Zone Bill.

— The ALP, with Prime Minister Bob Hawke, won reelection in Australia.

— The NZLP, with Prime Minister David Lange, won reelection in New Zealand.

Source: Much of this information was extracted from Dora Alves, *Anti-nuclear Attitudes in New Zealand and Australia* (Washington, D.C.: National Defense University, 1985).

Selected Bibliography

Government Documents, Messages, and Other Publications

American Embassy, Canberra. Telegram, subject: Foreign Minister Hayden's Arrival Statement in Wellington, 100320Z December 1986.

"ANZUS." *Background Briefs for Minister of Defence*. Wellington: New Zealand Ministry of Defence, July 1984.

"Australian Security Assistance Program." (U) Headquarters Pacific Air Forces, Plans and Policies Directorate, background paper. Hickam AFB, Hawaii, 26 February 1987. (Secret) Information extracted is unclassified.

Cleveland, Paul M. "U.S.-New Zealand Relations: Some Parting Observations." *Department of State Bulletin* 89, no. 2147 (Washington, D.C.: Government Printing Office, June 1989): 45-48.

"Current Defence Policies: Background." *Background Briefs for Minister of Defence*. Wellington: New Zealand Ministry of Defence, July 1984.

Defence Committee of Enquiry. *Defence and Security: What New Zealanders Want*. Wellington, New Zealand: V. R. Ward, Government Printer, 31 July 1986.

The Defence of Australia 1987. Canberra, Australia: Australian Government Publishing Service, March 1987.

Defence of New Zealand: Review of Defence Policy 1987. Wellington, New Zealand: V. R. Ward, Government Printer, February 1987.

The Defence Question: A Discussion Paper Issued as Background to the Public Submission on Future New Zealand Strategic and Security Policies. Wellington, New Zealand: V. R. Ward, Government Printer, December 1985.

Dibb, Paul. *Review of Australia's Defence Capabilities: Report to the Minister for Defence*. Canberra: Australian Government Publishing Service, March 1986.

Jackson, Karl D. US deputy assistant secretary of defense for East Asia and Pacific Affairs. Statement in House Committee on Foreign Affairs, *United States Policy toward New Zealand and Australia and the Current State of ANZUS: Hearings before the Subcommittee on Asian and Pacific Affairs*, 99th Cong., 2d sess., 25 September 1986.

Lilley, James R. US deputy assistant secretary of state for East Asia and Pacific Affairs. Statement in House Committee on Foreign Affairs. *United States Policy toward New Zealand and Australia and the Current State of ANZUS: Hearings before the Subcommittee on Asian and Pacific Affairs*, 99th Cong., 2d sess., 25 September 1986.

National Research Bureau. *Public Opinion Poll on Defence and Security: What New Zealanders Want*, annex to the Report of the Defence Committee of Enquiry. Wellington, New Zealand: V. R. Ward, Government Printer, July 1986.

"New Zealand Force, South East Asia." *Background Briefs for Minister of Defence.* Wellington: New Zealand Ministry of Defence, July 1984.

"Opening the Books." *Background Briefs for Minister of Defence.* Wellington: New Zealand Ministry of Defence, July 1984.

Organization of the Joint Chiefs of Staff. *United States Military Posture for FY 1987.* Washington, D.C.: Department of Defense, Summer 1986.

"Section 11—Defence." *New Zealand Official Yearbook—1985.* Wellington, New Zealand: V. R. Ward, Government Printer, 1985.

Shultz, George P. "On Alliance Responsibility." *Department of State Bulletin* 85, no. 2012 (September 1985): 33-37.

Solarz, Stephen J. US chairman, Subcommittee on Asian and Pacific Affairs. Opening statement in House Committee on Foreign Affairs. *United States Policy toward New Zealand and Australia and the Current State of ANZUS: Hearings before the Subcommittee on Asian and Pacific Affairs,* 99th Cong., 2d sess., 25 September 1986.

"Statement by the Minister for Defence: The Hon. Kim C. Beazley, MP, on Defence Initiatives in the South Pacific." 20 February 1987.

United States Information Service, American Embassy, Wellington. Telegram, subject: Media Reaction, 110351Z December 1986.

"USAF-RAAF Airman-to-Airman Talks." (U) Headquarters USAF, Deputy Chief of Staff, Plans, issue paper, 16 October 1986. Information extracted is unclassified.

US Department of State. Telegram, subject: Revised Transcript of Joint San Francisco Press Conference, 230606Z August 1986.

_____. Telegram, subject: Secretary's Statements at San Francisco, 152332Z August 1986.

"U.S.-New Zealand Disagreement on Port Access for U.S. Ships." *Department of State Bulletin* 86, no. 2114 (September 1986): 87.

"WESTCOM Expanded Relations Program." Headquarters US Western Command, information paper, Fort Shafter, Hawaii, 19 February 1987.

Wolfowitz, Paul D. "The ANZUS Alliance." *Current Policy,* no. 674, 18 March 1985.

_____. "The ANZUS Relationship: Alliance Management." *Current Policy,* no. 592, 24 June 1984.

Books/Monographs

Albinski, Henry S. *ANZUS: The United States and Pacific Security.* Lanham, Md.: University Press of America, 1987.

_____. *The Australian-American Security Relationship: A Regional and International Perspective.* St. Lucia, Australia: University of Queensland Press, 1981.

_____. *Politics and Foreign Policy in Australia: The Impact of Vietnam and Conscription.* Durham, N.C.: Duke University Press, 1970.

Alves, Dora. *Anti-nuclear Attitudes in New Zealand and Australia.* Washington, D.C.: National Defense University Press, 1985.

_____. *The ANZUS Partners.* Significant Issue Series, 6, no. 8. Washington, D.C.: Center for Strategic and International Studies, Georgetown University, 1984.

Babbage, Ross. *Rethinking Australia's Defence.* St. Lucia, Australia: University of Queensland Press, 1980.

"Defense Forces of Australia." *Military Balance 1987-88.* New York: Garden City Press, 1987.

"Defense Forces of New Zealand." *Military Balance 1987-88.* New York: Garden City Press, 1987.

Dibb, Paul, ed. *Australia's External Relations in the 1980s: The Interaction of Economic, Political, and Strategic Factors.* Canberra, Australia: Croom Helm, 1983.

Hastings, P. D. "Australian Regional Defence Co-operation in the 1980s." In *Australian Defence Policy for the 1980s,* eds. Robert O'Neill and D. M. Horner. St. Lucia, Australia: University of Queensland Press, 1982.

Henderson, John. "New Zealand Foreign Policy," in *New Zealand and the Pacific,* ed. Roderick Alley. Boulder, Colo.: Westview Press, 1984.

Kavanagh, Brian L. *The Changing Western Alliance in the South Pacific.* Maxwell AFB, Ala.: Air University Press, 1987.

Keneally, Thomas. *Outback.* London: Rand-McNally Publishing Company, 1983.

Mandle, William F. *Going It Alone: Australia's National Identity in the Twentieth Century.* Melbourne, Australia: The Penguin Press, 1977.

McKinley, Michael. "Divergence in Australia-New Zealand Security Relations," in *Security, Strategy, and Policy Responses in the Pacific Rim,* eds. Lawrence E. Grinter and Young Whan Kihl. Boulder, Colo.: Lynne Rienner Publishers, 1989, 221-38.

Spender, Sir Percy C. *Exercises in Diplomacy: The ANZUS Treaty and the Columbo Plan.* New York: New York University Press, 1969.

Starke, J. G. *The ANZUS Treaty Alliance.* Melbourne, Australia: Melbourne University Press, 1965.

Templeton, Malcolm. *Defence and Security: What New Zealand Needs.* Wellington, New Zealand: Institute of Policy Studies, Victoria University, 1986.

Wright, Vernon. *David Lange Prime Minister.* Wellington, New Zealand: Unwin Paperbacks, 1984.

Conference Papers/Unpublished Theses and Dissertations

Alves, Dora. "Strategic Imperatives to Strengthen the Fabric of Peace in the Pacific." Paper presented at a security conference on Strategic Imperatives and Western Responses in the Pacific. Sydney, Australia, 9-12 February 1986.

Babbage, Ross. "The Future of the Australian-New Zealand Defence Relationship." Paper presented at a seminar on New Zealand Defence Policy. Institute of Policy Studies, Victoria University, Wellington, New Zealand, 9 December 1986.

_____. "The Prospects for Security Cooperation between ANZUS Allies till the Turn of the Century." Paper presented at the National Defense University Conference on Pacific Basin Security: Impact of Political and Social Change toward Year 2000. Honolulu, Hawaii, 27 February 1987.

Burnett, Alan. "ANZUS Triangle: Defence and Security." n. p., 1978.

_____. "The Discontinuous Triangle." n. p., 1978.

Clements, Kevin P. "New Zealand Defence Policy Challenges for the Future." Paper presented at a seminar on New Zealand Defence Policy. Institute of Policy Studies, Victoria University, Wellington, New Zealand, 9 December 1986.

Davidson, John. "Security and Lines of Communication in the Pacific and Indian Oceans." Paper presented at the National Defense University Symposium on Pacific Security. Washington, D.C., 20 May 1981.

Gelber, Harry G. "Australian Strategic Perspectives." Paper presented at the National Defense University Symposium on Trans-Pacific Security Issues. Honolulu, Hawaii, 29 May 1980 (updated in October 1980).

Jamieson, Sir D. Ewan. "New Zealand Defence Policy: A Professional Viewpoint." Paper presented at a seminar on New Zealand Defence Policy. Institute of Policy Studies, Victoria University, Wellington, New Zealand, 9 December 1986.

Mediansky, Fedor A. "Threat Perception in the Southwest Pacific Region: An Australian Perspective." Paper presented at the National Defense University Conference on Pacific Basin Security: Impact of Political and Social Change toward Year 2000. Honolulu, Hawaii, 26 February 1987.

Riley, Philip. Draft research paper on New Zealand-American defense relations for the National War College research requirement. National War College, Ft. McNair, Washington, D.C., January 1987.

Shubert, Thomas W. "The United States and the Southwest Pacific: Policy Options for a Changing Region." Master's thesis, Naval Postgraduate School, Monterey, Calif., March 1986.

Templeton, Malcolm. "A Layman's Perspective." Paper presented at a seminar on New Zealand Defence Policy. Institute of Policy Studies, Victoria University, Wellington, New Zealand, 9 December 1986.

West, Dalton A. "New Zealand Security Perspective." Paper presented at a seminar on Strategic Imperatives and Western Responses in the Pacific. Sydney, Australia, 9-12 February 1986.

Young, Thomas-Durell. "An Analysis and Commentary: The Australian, New Zealand, and United States Defence Relationship, 1951-1986." PhD diss., University of Geneva, 1987.

_____. "Problems in Future New Zealand Defence Policy." n. p., December 1986.

_____. "United States Security Interests and Objectives." Paper presented at a seminar on Strategic Imperatives and Western Responses in the Pacific. Sydney, Australia, 9-12 February 1986.

Journals

Albinski, Henry S. "American Perspectives on the ANZUS Alliance." *Australian Outlook* 32, no. 2 (August 1978): 130-52.

_____. "Australia and New Zealand in the 1980s." *Current History* 85, no. 510 (April 1986): 149-82.

_____. "Australia and the United States: Appraisal of the Relationship." *Australian Journal of Politics and History* 29, no. 2 (1983): 288-300.

Alves, Dora. "Sea Change in the New Pacific." *Defense & Foreign Affairs* 15, no. 6 (June 1987): 38-43.

Ansell, Graham. "ANZUS Stand Explained." *New Zealand Foreign Affairs Review* 35, no. 1 (January-March 1985): 47-50.

"Anti-nuclear Bill Introduced." *New Zealand Foreign Affairs Review* 35, no. 4 (October-December 1985): 4-5.

Barclay, Glen St. John. "The Future of Australian-American Relations." *Australian Outlook* 30, no. 3 (December 1976): 459-73.

Bergin, Anthony. "Asian Security in Australian Perspective." *Asian Defence Journal*, October 1985, 70-84.

Boston, Jonathan. "The Fourth Labour Government in New Zealand: The Economics and Politics of Liberalization." *Australian Quarterly* 59, nos. 3/4 (Spring and Summer 1987): 366-76.

Brand, Robert A. "Australia, New Zealand, and ANZUS." The *Atlantic Community Quarterly* 22, no. 4 (Winter 1984-1985): 345-59.

Bridge, T. D. "Australian Defence under Hawke." *Army Quarterly and Defence Journal*, April 1984, 148-52.

Collins, Hugh. "Australia and the United States: Assessing the Relationship." *Australian Outlook* 32, no. 2 (August 1978): 153-68.

Cuddy, Dennis L. "The American Role in Australian Involvement in the Vietnam War." *The Australian Journal of Politics and History* 28, no. 3 (1982): 340-53.

Dalrymple, F. Rawdon. "On Being a Superpower's Ally: The Case of Australia." *Australian Foreign Affairs Record* 57, no. 7 (July 1987): 582-87.

Dibb, Paul. "Issues in Australian Defence." *Australian Outlook* 36, no. 3 (December 1983): 160-66.

Dorrance, John C. "ANZUS: Misperceptions, Mythology and Reality." *Australian Quarterly* 57, no. 3 (Spring 1985): 215-30.

Fisher, Richard D. "Responding to New Zealand's Challenge to Western Security in the South Pacific." *Backgrounder*, no. 48. The Heritage Foundation, Washington, D.C., 24 July 1986.

_____. "Why the U.S. Must Oppose the South Pacific Nuclear Free Zone." *Backgrounder*, no. 55. The Heritage Foundation, Washington, D.C., 23 December 1986.

Gelber, Harry G. "Australia, the United States and the Strategic Balance: Some Comments on the Joint Facilities." *Australian Outlook* 36, no. 2 (August 1982): 12-21.

Harland, Bryce. "A Continuing Partnership." *New Zealand Foreign Affairs Review* 35, no. 2 (April-June 1985): 25-29.

Harries, Owen. "Crisis in the Pacific." *Commentary*, June 1985, 47-54.

Hawkins, T. M. "Public Perceptions of Defence in Australia." *Journal of the Royal United Services Institute*, June 1985, 12-15.

"Industry Update." *Journal of Defense & Diplomacy* 7, no. 12 (December 1989): 5.

Laking, Sir George. "Assault on Economic Dependence." *New Zealand Financial Review*, December 1986, 7-8.

Lange, David. "Calling a Dead Letter a Dead Letter." *New Zealand International Review* 14, no. 4 (July/August 1989): 23-26.

_____. "New Interests, New Paths." *New Zealand Foreign Affairs Review* 35, no. 2 (April-June 1985): 10-16.

_____. "New Zealand's Security Policy." *Foreign Affairs* 63, no. 5 (Summer 1985): 1010-19.

_____. "Nuclear Policy Sparks Debate." *New Zealand Foreign Affairs Review* 35, no. 1 (January-March 1985): 3-17.

_____. "Relations with the United States." *New Zealand Foreign Affairs Review* 35, no. 3 (July-September 1985): 29-35.

Mack, Andrew. "Australia's Defense Revolution." *Journal of Defense & Diplomacy* 4, no. 9 (September 1986): 4-5.

_____. "Crisis in the Other Alliance: ANZUS in the 1980s." *World Policy Journal* 3, no. 3 (Summer 1986): 447-72.

_____. "U.S. Bases in Australia: The Controversy Grows." *Asian Defence Journal*, November 1984, 49-53.

McDougall, Derek. "The Hawke Government's Policies towards the USA." *The Round Table*, no. 310 (April 1989): 169.

Mediansky, Fedor A. "ANZUS in Crisis." *Australian Quarterly* 57, nos. 1 and 2 (Autumn/Winter 1985): 7-20.

_____. "Australia's Security and the American Alliance." *Australian Outlook*, April 1983, 22-25.

_____. "Australia's Security Outlook and the American Alliance." *Asian Defence Journal*, October 1986, 44-57.

_____. "The United States and Australia: Some Comments on a Reflection." *Australian Outlook* 31, no. 1 (April 1977): 121-23.

_____. "United States Interests in Australia." *Australian Outlook* 30, no. 1 (April 1976): 136-54.

Millar, T. B. "The Defence of Australia." *Daedalus* 114, no. 1 (Winter 1985): 259-79.

Millhouse, J. L. "Australia's Security beyond the Year 2000—The Importance of Asian-Pacific Economic Cooperation." *Journal of the Royal United Services Institute*, November 1984, 31-40.

O'Connor, Michael. "Australia's Defence Policy: Making the Facts Fit the Conclusion." *Asian Defence Journal*, June 1986, 4-14.

_____. "Australia's Regional Defence Cooperation." *Asian Defence Journal*, August 1985, 93-97.

_____. "Australia's Retreat into Isolationism." *Asian Defence Journal*, December 1982, 75-77.

O'Flynn, Frank. "Formidable Challenges for All." *New Zealand Foreign Affairs Review* 35, no. 2 (April-June 1985): 17-24.

Purcell, Gerald L. "The Value and Future of the ANZUS Alliance." *Journal of the Australian Naval Institute* 11, no. 1 (February 1985): 9-15.

Samuel, Peter. "The Dibb Report and Australia's Defense Vagaries." *Strategic Review* 14, no. 4 (Fall 1986): 47-53.

Samuel, Peter, and P. F. Serong. "The Troubled Waters of ANZUS." *Strategic Review* 14, no. 1 (Winter 1986): 39-48.

Siracusa, Joseph M. "Australian-American Relations, 1980: A Historical Perspective." *Orbis* 24, no. 2 (Summer 1980): 271-87.

Siracusa, Joseph M., and Glen St. John Barclay. "Australia, the United States, and the Cold War, 1945-51: From V-J Day to ANZUS." *Diplomatic History* 5, no. 1 (1981): 39-52.

_____. "Further Reflections on United States Interests in Australia." *Australian Outlook* 30, no. 3 (December 1976): 474-79.

Sunderland, Ray. "What Is Australia's Defence Strategy?" *Journal of the Royal United Services Institute*, November 1984, 11-16.

Thakur, Ramesh. "A Nuclear Weapon-Free South Pacific: A New Zealand Perspective." *Pacific Affairs* 58, no. 2 (Summer 1985): 216-38.

_____. "New Zealand and ANZUS: From Milestone to Millstone?" *Asian Defence Journal*, December 1984, 12-17.

_____. "New Zealand: In Search of a Defence Policy." *Asian Defence Journal*, July 1985, 52-60.

Thana, S. "Australia's Defence Perspectives: A Review on the Way." *Asian Defence Journal*, April 1984, 57-81.

Tow, William T. "ANZUS and American Security." *Survival* 23, no. 6 (1981): 261-71.

"U.S. Terminates ANZUS Treaty with New Zealand." *Atlantic Community News*, Summer 1986, 2.

White, B. "The Defence Link across the Tasman." *Journal of the Royal United Services Institute*, November 1984, 60-67.

Young, P. Lewis. "ANZUS: Politics of an Alliance." *Asian Defence Journal*, December 1982, 66-71.

_____. "Australian Defense Minister Emphasizes Self-Reliance and Cooperative Programs." *Armed Forces Journal International*, November 1989, 44-45.

_____. "Estrangement from US Cuts New Zealand's Defense Options." *Armed Forces Journal International*, June 1989, 52.

_____. "Project Jindalee: Australia's OTH Backscatter Radar." *Asian Defence Journal*, February 1985, 58-62.

_____. "The RNZAF: Tough Going Ahead." *Asian Defence Journal*, August 1985, 76-81.

Young, Thomas-Durell. "Down Under White Papers." *US Naval Institute Proceedings* 114, no. 3 (March 1988): 136-44.

_____. "New Zealand Air Power Requirements and Force Determinants." *Air University Review* 37, no. 3 (March-April 1986): 82-92.

_____. "New Zealand Defence Policy under Labour." *Naval War College Review* 39, no. 3 (May-June 1986): 22-34.

_____. "New Zealand's Dilemmas." US Naval Institute *Proceedings* 111, no. 8 (August 1985): 51-56.

_____. "Problems in Australia's 'Defense Revolution.'" *Contemporary Southeast Asia* 11, no. 3 (December 1989): 237-56.

_____. "'Self-Reliance' and Force Development in the RAN." US Naval Institute *Proceedings* 112, no. 3 (March 1986): 157-62.

Magazines and Other Sources

Alves, Dora. "A Meaningful Maritime Strategy for Australia." *Pacific Defence Reporter* 13, no. 3 (September 1986): 9-11.

Ashworth, N. F. "Time, Gentlemen, Please." *Pacific Defence Reporter* 12, no. 12 (June 1986): 14-15.

Babbage, Ross. "Implications of Dibb Report for Defence Industry." *Pacific Defence Reporter* 13, no. 3 (September 1986): 35.

Barnes, F. W. "F/A-18 a Major Plus, But Little Progress in Real Defence." *Pacific Defence Reporter* 12, nos. 6/7 (December 1985-January 1986): 224-27.

Barnett, David. "Officers March from a Dilapidated Force." *The Bulletin* 108, no. 5539 (7 October 1986): 26-29.

_____. "Substance or Symbolism: The Dilemma for Radical Hawke." *The Bulletin* 108, no. 5514 (15 April 1986): 26-30.

Beaglehole, John H. "No 1—New Zealand: The End of an Era." *Pacific Defence Reporter* 11, no. 10 (April 1985): 8-10.

_____. "Labor's Dangerous New Course." *Pacific Defence Reporter* 12, nos. 6/7 (December 1985-January 1986): 14-16.

_____. "New Zealand's Defence: The Year of Debate." *Pacific Defence Reporter* 10, nos. 6/7 (December 1983-January 1984): 75-85.

_____. "New Zealand Wants to Eat Its Cake and Have It, Too." *Pacific Defence Reporter* 11, no. 3 (September 1984): 22-62.

"Big Man from a Small Place." *The Bulletin* 108, no. 5500 (7 January 1986): 58.

Brand, Robert A. "Defence Down Under: An American View." *Pacific Defence Reporter* 11, no. 12 (June 1985): 11-14.

Clark, Andrew. "Hawke Gets the Message that American Farmers Come First." *The Bulletin* 108, no. 5516 (29 April 1986): 24-26.

_____. "Lange Symbolism Exacerbates ANZUS Schism." *The Bulletin* 108, no. 5521 (3 June 1986): 1.

Confidential discussions with officials in the US Department of Defense, US State Department, Australian Embassy, and New Zealand Embassy in Washington, D.C.,

January 1987; and officials in the military headquarters representing all the US military services on Oahu, Hawaii, March 1987.

Crowe, William J. "No 17—The US Cannot, and Should Not, Go It Alone." *Pacific Defence Reporter* 12, no. 2 (August 1985): 11-16.

"Defence and Industry: A New Deal." *The Bulletin* 108, no. 5526 (8 July 1986): 71-72.

"Defence White Paper." *Pacific Defence Reporter* 13, no. 10 (April 1987): 19-23.

Edwards, John. "How We Can Defend Ourselves." *The Bulletin* 108, no. 5517 (6 May 1986): 52-56.

_____. "Secret Report: We'll Go It Alone with Fast, Hit-hard Forces." *The Bulletin* 108, no. 5513 (8 April 1986): 24-28.

Grazebrook, A. W. "The RAN: The Decline Continues." *Pacific Defence Reporter* 12, nos. 6/7 (December 1985-January 1986): 219-22.

_____. "No 2—Errors of Major Significance." *Pacific Defence Reporter* 13, no. 2 (August 1986): 19-20.

_____. "No 2—The Navy No Longer a Credible Force." *Pacific Defence Reporter* 10, nos. 6/7 (December 1983-January 1984): 251-55.

Griggs, Tim. "Australia: New Security Perspectives and Policies." *International Defense Review* 19, no. 5 (May 1986): 579-80.

"The Growing Watchful Eye on Our North." *The Bulletin* 108, no. 5553 (20 January 1987): 53-56.

Gwynn-Jones, Terry. "The Royal Australian Air Force." *Air Force Magazine* 68, no. 8 (August 1985): 66-70.

Hamilton, Ian. "No 1—Most Testing Period Ahead." *Pacific Defence Reporter* 13, nos. 6/7 (December 1986-January 1987): 199-200.

Handleman, Howard. "Whither Australia? U.S. Has Major Reservations about Dibb Report." *Pacific Defence Reporter* 13, no. 2 (August 1986): 45.

Henderson, Peter. "Isolationist Trends in Dibb Report." *Pacific Defence Reporter* 13, no. 3 (September 1986): 8-9.

Inder, Stuart. "The Unsqueaky Facing up to Charles Atlas." *The Bulletin* 109, no. 5560 (10 March 1987): 35-36.

Jamieson, Sir D. Ewan. "Defence Dilemmas of Small Countries in the Nuclear Age." *Pacific Defence Reporter* 13, no. 5 (November 1986): 40-41.

Jordan, Robert P. "New Zealand: The Last Utopia." *National Geographic* 171, no. 5 (May 1987): 654-81.

Keys, Henry. "Why Australia Build Is Worth the Extra Cost: The New Submarine Project." *Pacific Defence Reporter* 13, no. 3 (September 1986): 38-39.

McNamara, Sir Neville. "No 1—A Serious Guide to Future Defence." *Pacific Defence Reporter* 13, no. 4 (October 1986): 32-34.

Mediansky, Fedor A. "Washington Startled by a Roaring Mouse Down Under." *The Bulletin* 108, no. 5544 (11 November 1986): 118-20.

Muir, Tom. "Submarines and Self-Reliance." *The Bulletin* 108, no. 5526 (8 July 1986): 75-76.

_____. "The US-ANZUS Partner and Major Defence Supplier." *Pacific Defence Reporter* 12, no. 10 (April 1986): 12-13.

_____. "Vicissitudes and Achievements in Defence Offsets Program." *Pacific Defence Reporter* 12, no. 10 (April 1986): 1-10.

O'Connor, Michael. "Dibb's Siege Mentality: The Counter View." *The Bulletin* 108, no. 5526 (8 July 1986): 67-72.

_____. "Fundamental Weaknesses in Australia's Defence Policy." *Pacific Defence Reporter* 12, nos. 6/7 (December 1985-January 1986): 213-14.

Richardson, Michael. "Labor under Pressure to Change on ANZUS." *Pacific Defence Reporter* 13, no. 9 (March 1987): 35-36.

Robertson, Andrew. "Wars Not Won by Defence Alone." *Pacific Defence Reporter* 13, no. 3 (September 1986): 13-15.

Robertson, Frank. "Pine Gap Raises Its Outer Veil." *Pacific Defence Reporter* 12, no. 10 (April 1986): 14-15.

Roome, Jack V. "Soviet Military Expansion in the Pacific." *Pacific Defence Reporter* 13, no. 2 (August 1986): 12-14.

Smollowe, Jill. "Pacific Overtures: Moscow's Moves in the Far East Worry Washington." *Time* 128, no. 20 (17 November 1986): 58-59.

Special Correspondent. "No 3: RAAF Happiest of Defence Forces." *Pacific Defence Reporter* 10, nos. 6/7 (December 1983-January 1984): 257-58.

Stackhouse, John. "Defence Brass Prepare for Infighting." *The Bulletin* 108, no. 5513 (8 April 1986): 26-27.

_____. "Defence 86—Going It Alone." *The Bulletin* 108, no. 5526 (8 July 1986): 52-67.

_____. "The Dibb Repellent." *The Bulletin* 108, no. 5523 (17 June 1986): 26-27.

_____. "A Glimpse at a Growing Pine Gap." *The Bulletin* 108, no. 5507 (25 February 1986): 51-52.

_____. "New Subs Survive Attack." *The Bulletin* 109, no. 5560 (10 March 1987): 56-58.

Stevenson, J. D. "Army—Skilled, Dedicated, But Denied Adequate Means." *Pacific Defence Reporter* 12, nos. 6/7 (December 1985-January 1986): 216-18.

_____. "A High-Quality Army, But No Means to Do the Job." *Pacific Defence Reporter* 10, nos. 6/7 (December 1983-January 1984): 248-49.

_____. "Is the Defence Force Effective?" *Pacific Defence Reporter* 15, nos. 6/7 (December 1988-January 1989): 227-30.

_____. "The Logistic Problem: It Must Be Faced." *Pacific Defence Reporter* 10, no. 8 (February 1983): 22-24.

_____. "No 2—Logistic Support Demands More Attention." *Pacific Defence Reporter* 13, no. 4 (October 1986): 35-48.

Street, Tony. "Alliances, Threats and the World Around Us: No 1—Why Australia Is Aligned." *Pacific Defence Reporter* 9, no. 8 (February 1983): 8-12.

Synnot, Sir Anthony. "No 1—Basic Strategy Is Wrong." *Pacific Defence Reporter* 13, no. 2 (August 1986): 17-18.

Templeton, Ian. "Lange Moving to Make Australia a Brother in Arms." *The Bulletin* 108, no. 5541 (21 October 1986): 110.

_____. "Minister at War with Generals Shoots PM's Toe." *The Bulletin* 107, no. 5505 (11 February 1986): 82.

_____. "Wellington Ponders Post-ANZUS Pacific Security." *The Bulletin* 108, no. 5519 (20 May 1986): 104-5.

"Tough Recovery—New Zealand." *The Economist* 304, no. 7506 (11 July 1987): 69-70.

Varni, Gerald. "ICA Exclusive Interview—The Honorable Kim Beazley, Australia's Minister of Defense." *International Combat Arms* 5, no. 2 (March 1987): 80-82.

Warner, Denis. "No 2—'New Zealand Can't Have It Both Ways.'" *Pacific Defence Reporter* 11, no. 10 (April 1985): 12-15.

_____. "The Importance of Being ANZUS." *Pacific Defence Reporter* 11, no. 3 (September 1984): 19-21.

_____. "Soviet Union Not Just a Country, But a Cause." *Pacific Defence Reporter* 12, no. 10 (April 1986): 8-10.

Weinberger, Caspar W. "We Would Welcome New Zealand's Return Anytime." *Pacific Islands Monthly* 56, no. 12 (December 1985): 18-21.

_____. "The Five Pillars of Our Defense Policy in East Asia and the Pacific." *Defense 84*, no. 23 (April 1984): 2-7.

Williams, Clive. "Better to Deter than to Defend." *Pacific Defence Reporter* 12, no. 12 (June 1986): 17-20.

Young, P. Lewis. "International Defense Profile: Australian Defense Forces." *International Combat Arms* 5, no. 2 (March 1987): 67-79.

Young, Thomas-Durell. "Australia's Defense Priorities and Programs." *International Defense Review* 19, no. 5 (May 1986): 583-88.

_____. "Don't Abandon Radford-Collins." *Pacific Defence Reporter* 13, no. 3 (September 1986): 16.

_____. "New Zealand's Defense Arrangements: An Uncertain Period Ahead." *International Defense Review* 19, no. 5 (May 1986): 591-94.

_____. "Problems in Future New Zealand Defence Policy." n. p., December 1986, 1-14.

Newspapers

Andrews, B. "Admiral Points to Soviet Fish Pact." *Washington Times*, 11 September 1986, 4D.

Barber, David. "New Zealand Takes Ambitious Tack with New Defense Policy." *Christian Science Monitor*, 30 March 1987.

Brownfeld, Allan C. "Fragility of Alliance Illustrated in New Zealand." *Washington Times*, 12 September 1984, 3C-4C.

Dyer, Gwynne. "New Zealand's Pesky Nix on Nukes." *Washington Times*, 1 November 1984, 3C.

"Fiji Coup to Block Indian Power." *Pittsburgh Press*, 17 May 1987, 7A.

Fulghum, David. "Foreign Officers Study Dynamics of Alliances." *Air Force Times*, 8 December 1986, 49.

Haberman, Clyde. "Challenge in the Pacific." *New York Times*, 7 September 1986, 26-113.

Hays, Ronald J. "Soviet Shadow Is Apparent in Pacific Security Setting." *San Diego Union*, 10 August 1986, 6C-10C.

Matthews, William. "New Zealand to Lose DoD Military Purchasing Help." *Air Force Times*, 9 March 1987, 36.

"New Zealand Military Says Standards Slip since U.S. Break." *New York City Tribune*, 2 October 1986, 3.

"New Zealand's New Leader Reiterates Labor Party's Antinuclear Stance." *Washington Post*, 20 July 1984, 28.

"New Zealand Parliament Asked to Ban Nuclear Arms." *Washington Times*, 13 February 1987, 9.

Pound, Kate. "Aussies, Americans Test Air Tactics in Kangaroo '89." *Pacific Stars and Stripes*, 24 August 1989, 8.

Ross, Oakland. "South Pacific Shakes Fist at the U.S." *Toronto Globe & Mail*, 25 October 1986, 3D.

Samuel, Peter. "New Zealand Anti-Nuclear View Driving U.S. Naval Operations to Australia." *New York City Tribune*, 11 March 1987, 5.

_____. "Soviets Buying Access to Strategic South Pacific Islands, Baker Tells Congress." *Defense News*, 29 September 1986, 13.

_____. "Weinberger Criticizes Report Recommending Australian Defense Policy Changes." *Defense News*, 10 November 1986, 28.

Sherwell, Chris. "Jindalee Takes Australian Defence by Storm." *Financial Times*, 10 February 1987, 4.

"Troop Withdrawal." *Washington Times*, 19 January 1987, 3(20).

"U.S. Hopes Nuclear Policy Will Exit with Lange." *Washington Times*, 8 August 1989, 7.

"Whither the Alliance?" *Air Force Times*, 9 February 1987, 28.

Young, Peter. "Marching in the Right Direction." *The Australian*, 7 January 1987, 1.

Index

Index